Recipes from

MY RUSSIAN GRANDMOTHER'S KITCHEN

Recipes from

MY RUSSIAN GRANDMOTHER'S KITCHEN

Discover the rich and varied character of Russian cuisine in 60 traditional dishes

ELENA MAKHONKO

WITH PHOTOGRAPHS BY JON WHITAKER

LORENZ BOOKS

This edition is published by Lorenz Books
an imprint of Anness Publishing Ltd
info@anness.com
www.lorenzbooks.com
www.annesspublishing.com

If you like the images in this book
and would like to investigate using
them for publishing, promotions or
advertising, please visit our website
www.practicalpictures.com for
more information.

A CIP catalogue record for this book
is available from the British Library.

Publisher: Joanna Lorenz
Editorial Director: Helen Sudell
Executive Editor: Joanne Rippin
Photography: Jon Whitaker
Food Stylist: Jenny White
Prop Stylist: Penny Markham
Designer: Adelle Morris
Production Controller: Ben Worley

NOTES
Bracketed terms are intended for
American readers. For all recipes,
quantities are given in both metric and
imperial measures and, where appropriate,
in standard cups and spoons. Follow
one set of measures, but not a mixture,
because they are not interchangeable.

Standard spoon and cup measures
are level. 1 tsp = 5ml, 1 tbsp = 15ml,
1 cup = 250ml/8fl oz.

Australian standard tablespoons are
20ml. Australian readers should use
3 tsp in place of 1 tbsp for measuring
small quantities.

American pints are 16fl oz/2 cups.
American readers should use 20fl oz/
2.5 cups in place of 1 pint when
measuring liquids.

Electric oven temperatures in this book
are for conventional ovens. When using a
fan oven, the temperature will probably
need to be reduced by about 10–20°C/
20–40°F. Since ovens vary, you should
check with your manufacturer's instruction
book for guidance.

The nutritional analysis given for each
recipe is calculated per portion (i.e. serving
or item), unless otherwise stated. If the
recipe gives a range, such as Serves 4–6,
then the nutritional analysis will be for the
smaller portion size, i.e. 6 servings.
The analysis does not include optional
ingredients, such as salt added to taste.

Medium (US large) eggs are used
unless otherwise stated.

Contents

Introduction

Russian recipes are passed through the generations, and cooking is taught from a young age. Most families follow their *babushka*'s (grandmother's) advice, and in this way each family has developed their own versions of typical Russian recipes. The dishes often originate from one of the fifteen former Soviet Republics, as well as from the regions within the Russian Federation, and all are dependent on the climate and geography of this vast country. Russians have always loved their cuisine, and the country has a lot to offer anybody interested in good food.

Mention Russian food, and most people will conjure up an image of a tureen of ruby-red borscht, warm blinis with melted butter, exclusive caviar from the Caspian Sea and maybe Beef Stroganoff or Chicken Kiev. But there is more – much more. A country as enormous as Russia has a lot to offer. Russians love to party and enjoy good food and drink with family and friends, and this has helped to foster a cuisine eminently worthy of recognition.

Food in a cold climate
Most of Russia is located north of the 51st latitude, and hence has a fairly cold climate all year round. Russians are used to the cold, and also to the scarcity of food during the winter months, and have developed all sorts of recipes for making filling dishes out of a few locally available ingredients.

RIGHT Russian winters are so severe that even the cities are covered in thick snow.

The Russian people have had to survive famines and lack of food repeatedly through history, whether this was caused by adverse weather conditions or by social conflict. During the Soviet era it was difficult to buy the ingredients for a decent meal, and there were only a few restaurants. However, since the fall of the Soviet system, Russian cuisine has exploded into life, and today there is interest in food among both old and young.

Culinary influences
A small part of Russia, officially the Russian Federation, lies within Europe, while the major part is part of Asia. Russia is the largest country in the world, from the Baltic in the west to the Bering Strait in the east, and there is a 10-hour time difference between eastern and western Russia. Norway, Finland, Estonia, Latvia, Belarus and Ukraine are the western neighbouring countries; Russia also borders Lithuania and Poland, Georgia and Azerbaijan in the south-west, with China, North Korea, Mongolia and Kazakhstan to the south.

Geography and landscape
The Russian coastline runs along the Japanese Sea, the Pacific Ocean, the White Sea and the Arctic Ocean. Russia is dependent on fishing as a source of income and has enormous fleets.

LEFT Golden autumn colours in Karachai, a part of Russia's Caucasus region.

The Caspian Sea is a salt lake and one of the largest and deepest in the world. It is considered to be one of the oldest lakes on earth and is the major breeding ground for sturgeon, the fish that gives the Russians their famous and much-loved caviar.

In ancient history people settled down along the many rivers and seas. There were plenty of fish to catch and a big variety of fish dishes have always been on the Russian tables. The rivers also serve as transport through the country, in particular the Volga, which is the longest river in Europe.

Russia is a country of contrasts and offers a great variety of climate and vegetation. Large areas are either too cold or too dry for agriculture, and there are large areas of the country where nothing at all can be grown. The taiga, south of the Arctic tundra, has long cold winters with only a couple of months of summer and this large forested area runs like a belt through the country.

A vast mountainous area in Eurasia, the Caucasus borders Iran to the south, Turkey to the south-west, the Black Sea to the west, the Caspian Sea to the east and Russia to the north. This region provides Russians with wheat, vegetables, herbs, fruits, honey and yogurt. Vineyards and orchards are abundant, and also olive groves in the warmer climate.

Eating in Russia
The first people to live in the vast country known today as Russia were nomadic hunters and fishermen, making use of all the natural resources available to feed their families. When people first made settlements, farming and animal herding became the main source of food. Rye, wheat and cabbage were staple foods and learning the technique of preserving them during

ABOVE Lake Darashkol, in the dramatic and beautiful Siberian mountain range.

the cold winter months became a matter of life or death. From this necessity arose many delicious recipes for pickled and preserved foods that are still in use today.

The northern part of Russia is very sparsely populated, even now. Here time stands still and life in the area is very harsh. Meat is a rarity and enjoyed only on special occasions. People eat much the same food as they have always done: bread, root vegetables, dairy products and fish.

Russian recipes
When talking about Russian cuisine it is necessary to include the whole of the former Soviet Union, because the different regions have contributed to the diversity of Russian cuisine for centuries. Some of the exquisite national dishes are Chicken Kiev from Ukraine, exotic Pilaff from Uzbekistan, Pelmeni from Siberia, and the garlic-fragrant Harcho from Georgian. These are as common on the Russian dinner table as Beef Stroganoff or Koulibiac, and it would be unforgivable not to include them in a Russian cookbook.

This book reflects the rich diversity of a unique cuisine and celebrates the central position food maintains in Russia. If you share the Russian love of hospitality you will enjoy sharing the delicious recipes in this book.

Russian food culture

The company of family and friends is just as important as the meal itself to most Russians. If there is no time during the week, they will make time for an afternoon of socializing during the weekend. Planning the recipes, shopping for the right ingredients, eating the food and discussing it afterwards are all vital elements of this social experience.

The cuisine of the past

Many years ago, this huge country had a largely rural population. The peasants would work on land owned by the nobility, and traditional methods of food production lasted for centuries. All kinds of grain, particularly wheat, corn and buckwheat, were grown on the wide, flat fields, and this encouraged the development of recipes for different kinds of bread, pastry and cakes. Little pies are a feature of *zakuski*, the array of little dishes to tempt the appetite, and bread is an absolute staple of the Russian diet – no meal would be complete without it.

Many Russians own a country cottage or a small piece land where they can grow vegetables, berries and fruits – apples are especially appreciated. When young people come to visit their parents at the cottage, they will most probably get homemade pastry, pirogi, to bring back home for the week ahead.

A pirogi can be filled with meat or vegetables as well as fruits or berries. The skill of a hostess is often judged by how well she makes pirogi, and in the past pirogi was sometimes used as an invitation for dinner.

21st-century changes

The hoarding instinct became more pronounced if anything in the food shortages during the 20th century, when Communism changed the way the land was farmed, not always for the better as far as feeding the people was concerned. When Communism fell in the late 20th century, a small but

influential new upper class appeared, the 'new Russians', along with a growing lower class whose access to wealth was strictly limited. The new Russians are affluent, sometimes super-wealthy, and this spending power has introduced a completely new spectrum of luxury items in the food stores as well as Western-style restaurants and coffee houses.

Tea and coffee houses

The Russians love their tea and after the perestroika era the tea trend has grown even stronger. One example is

ABOVE The interior of a typical up-market Russian tea room.

the exclusive chain of tea houses, Chai House, that serve white tea as one of many expensive tea brands. Tea parties at home are common and here tea and different sweets and cakes are served. At special occasions, a hostess might serve a magnificent cake with plenty of whipped cream and meringue, most likely bought in a *bulochnaya*, one of the grand old Russian bakeries that have beautiful crystal chandeliers hanging from the ceiling.

ABOVE The traditional loaves of Russian bread being baked in a Moscow bakery.

ABOVE Glasses of Russian beer at a Moscow restaurant table.

time. Casseroles and soups are made in large 7-litre pans and nobody thinks twice about eating the same food for four consecutive days.

A day's food

Breakfast is usually a cup of tea with sugar and a slice of lemon, and maybe a piece of bread or cake to go with it.

The classical Russian lunch is often taken in a *stolovaja*. These are simple cafeterias where students and employees eat an inexpensive lunch of genuine Russian food. Usually there are three courses to choose from, including a soup. As always in Russia bread and tea is served with the meal.

Dinner is the main meal of the day. In past times, when many people were working hard on the land, it would be a substantial affair to keep up the energy levels. The nobility stretched this meal into several courses, while peasants might be on basic rations of bread and soup, maybe with a little meat or fish.

These days, if it is a special occasion there will be some appetizers (zakuski), a thick, rich soup, a variety of small courses, or a main course of meat, fish or poultry. Desserts are usually light and based on fruit after the rich and substantial savoury courses.

BELOW A display of some of the many different kinds of dried fruit and nuts available in Danilovsky Market in Moscow.

Coffee is sold everywhere at all prices depending on what kind of coffee and place you are looking for. In a traditional coffee house it is very popular to have coffee with ice cream and champagne.

Restaurants

When Russians cook at home they do not think or care about which region the dish originates from, they just cook their favourite food. That is not the case when the meal is taken in a restaurant. A Georgian restaurant would never dream of serving a course from Ukraine.

Fast food

When McDonald's came to Russia it inspired the start of a whole wave of Russian fast food places. One of the biggest is Jolki-Palki, where a buffet of hot and cold traditional Russian courses are offered for a low price. Each fast food chain has its own speciality. The most perfect Russian fast food has really been around all the time, the pelmeni, which can be made with around 20 different fillings. Another Russian classic to be found on the streets of most towns is the beer

stand, the beer being served warm when the weather is cold, and always accompanied by a salty snack such as salted fish or boiled crayfish.

Shopping and cooking

Many Russians today shop at supermarkets, where they can buy typical Russian fare as well as imported delicacies. But special food market stalls entirely devoted to either pickled vegetables or many kinds of dried fruit, still thrive, while bread is usually bought from the baker.

The typical Russian way of cooking is to make large batches of food at one

Traditional dishes

The basic foods eaten every day in Russia are quite simple. The particular flavour of Russian food lies in the way the ingredients are combined, and the typical seasonings of herbs, salt, pepper and sour cream (smetana).

Pelmeni

These little pasta rolls, filled with meat and eaten all over Russia, are something between dim sum and ravioli and originally came from China.

Pelmeni are at their best when home-made, but these days they can be bought frozen. Making these snacks is a fantastic way of spending quality time with friends and family, as pelmeni are usually made in big batches, often around a hundred at a time. There is always a bottle of vodka and a plate of simple zakuski around to help yourself from while the baking goes on. One person takes care of the dough, another mixes the meat, and a third fills the little rolls with the filling. Once ready, the pelmeni are placed in perfect straight rows on cutting boards, carefully counted and placed in the freezer. They taste best 'frost-bitten', according to the Russians.

ABOVE Frost-bitten pelmeni ready to be dropped in boiling stock.

When it is time to eat, the pelmeni are boiled from frozen in water and stock, and served with refreshing sour smetana, a couple of drops of vinegar, salt and freshly ground black pepper – simple, yet elegant. Around 40 pelmeni per person is a normal portion, and vodka is the only possible drink to go with them.

Pastries – savoury and sweet

Savoury pastries are a meal in themselves, filled with meat, cabbage, mushrooms or onions. Sweet pastries contain fruit or berries and cottage cheese, and are a favourite snack with a cup of tea. There are all sorts of different specialities such as pirogi, pirogjki, kulebjaka and rastegaj, all made of the same kind of dough. Rastegaj means 'unbutton me', and they are served with soup spooned through the opening at the top.

LEFT Russian food at its most indulgent: smoked salmon and blinis with caviar.

ABOVE There are many different versions of the famous Russian or Ukrainian borscht.

Blinis – a symbol of life

Outside Russia blinis are small, thick, buckwheat pancakes, but Russians make their blinis with wheat and sometimes of oat flour. They are often as large and thin as the most delicate crêpes. For Russians, blinis have symbolized life and fertility since pagan times. Perfectly round, golden and warm, the blini also symbolizes the sun. During Maslenitsa, a happy festival where the return of the spring is celebrated, blinis are the main food for a whole week. They are also eaten to excess before the start of Lent.
In the old days they were served to women in childbirth to help them to gather their strength and sustain them through labour. 'Life begins and ends with blini', according to the Russians.

Soup – the centre of the meal

No other cuisine can present such a wide variety of soups as the Russian tradition. Russian soups are often thick and rich and every home has its own favourite and secret recipes, inherited from older generations. In Russia, soup is either served as the first course, or between the appetizer and the main course. Borscht, one of the most famous soups of the country, is said to come from Ukraine, but though Ukraine has a deserved reputation for making good soups, nobody can be sure of its true origin. As with other Russian soups there are many different recipes, the only ingredient that always stays the same is the beetroot (beet) that gives it its beautiful red colour.

Meat and fish – the main course

Russians are a meat-loving people and eat meat almost every day if they are not on a religious fast. Jarkoje, big pieces of meat fried on the stove, is popular. Another highly appreciated dish is sashlik, a kebab of barbecued meat, usually lamb or pork. When Russians invite guests for dinner the favourite main dish to serve is some kind of poultry.

With so many natural fishing waters, fish is bound to appear on the Russian dinner table. The wonderful variety of dishes is a remnant from the old days when everybody adhered to the fasting days of the religious calendar.

Beer, champagne and vodka

Russian beer is very popular and there are many brands to choose from. Baltika is the most common and well known.

Russian champagne is sweet and served at room temperature, but the new generation has learnt to appreciate French champagne the way Winston Churchill preferred it, 'Cold, dry and free'. Champagne is often served throughout a good dinner.

Vodka is made from wheat grain and is transparent. Western vodka is usually dry, whereas Russian vodka has

BELOW Meat or fish kebabs, cooked on huge outdoor fires, are a much-loved Russian eating tradition.

LEFT Russians love their vodkas, especially when served ice cold.

a touch of sweetness from sugar, berries or fruits. Roots and herbs are also used to season vodka. Chilli pepper vodka is bottled with a whole red chilli. Vodka is usually enjoyed straight, and Russians always have a piece of dark bread or a salted cucumber to go with it.

To have a toast with vodka is a way of showing respect for the host. The tradition is to empty the glass in a single gulp. There is a Russian saying, 'To leave vodka in the glass is to leave tear drops for the host'.

Tea

In the old days, tea was served from the sizzling samovar and drunk from cups of finest porcelain. Today electric kettles and tea bags are commonplace, but the samovar, also now likely to be an electric one, is still used at tea parties. Russians take sugar and a slice of lemon with their tea, rather than milk.

BELOW The samovar may have been replaced by the kettle, but it is still held in great affection by Russians.

Festivals and celebrations

The Russian festival year has followed the seasons and the rural way of life for centuries. Such traditions survive for a long time, and often an old tradition will turn into a new one. This happened when Orthodox Christianity became the main Russian religion, as far back as the first millennium, and many pagan festivals were transformed into religious ones to fit the Church calendar. The same thing happened again during the Soviet era when the Orthodox Church was abolished and the celebration of religious traditions was forbidden, but seasonal festivals and their accompanying food rituals survived under different names.

As in most countries, special recipes are connected to the various festivals, and these traditions have survived both the banning of religious holidays and the food shortages of the 20th century. Hospitality is very important in most Russian households, and food and drink must be offered to visitors as they arrive to celebrate any holiday. Even at christenings, when the focus is on the newborn baby and its acceptance into

BELOW A girl lights a candle in Our Lady of Kazan Cathedral in St Petersburg. The Orthodox church celebrates Christmas Day on 7 January.

the Church, no one would expect to leave without a glass of vodka and a plate or two of food.

New Year's Eve

According to the Julian calendar, New Year is in the beginning of January, before Christmas. During the years when Christmas was not celebrated, some of the activities that belonged to Christmas were transferred to the New Year celebration. The decorated fir tree and the Russian Santa Claus, Father Frost (*Ded Moroz*), now are part of the New Year celebrations. On New Year's Eve, 31 December, Russians like to

celebrate with a party drinking vodka and champagne and tasting all their favourite dishes from the zakuski table. At midnight there is more champagne and festive fireworks.

The New Year is the big party for the children. The highlight of the celebration is the arrival of Father Frost, accompanied by the beautiful Snow Maiden (*Snegurochka*). All year, the children have been told that if they do not behave, Father Frost will not bring them any presents, and many

BELOW New Year fireworks go off over the St. Basil's Cathedral in Red Square.

ABOVE A Russian swimmer takes an icy plunge on 19 January, to mark the Epiphany. The ice is so deep, holes have to be cut.

parents rent a Father Frost to come to their house and give him presents to hand out. A Father Frost may make ten visits during the evening. According to Russian tradition he is offered a glass of vodka at every place and cannot refuse without being rude. Father Frost carries a staff and wears a long blue coat, lined with leather or fur. His helper, the Snow Maiden represents the frozen rivers and lakes and is dressed in a sparkling blue gown.

Christmas

Orthodox Christians follow the Julian calendar so Christmas Day falls on 7 January, and is a quiet family celebration in comparison to the more extravagant New Year celebrations.

During the Soviet era it was actually forbidden to celebrate Christmas for several years. However, many people continued to celebrate in secret. Today Christmas once again is regarded as a religious festival and a national holiday. God returned to Russia after perestroika and the politicians now stand side by side with the people in

the church at Christmas Eve. Many people follow the tradition of fasting before Christmas when they will avoid dishes that contain fat and meat. Many traditional Russian dishes have been specifically created to be eaten during the fasting period, including the 'caviars' made from vegetables, especially beetroot (beet) and mushrooms. A meal of 13 of these dishes is eaten on Christmas Eve, one of which is kutja, a porridge made with honey and raisins that is also served at funerals. The meal begins with zakuski, after which there will be a borscht, or another rich soup. Pasties with mushrooms, fish or cabbage are served with the soup.

On Christmas Day the fast is over and a huge meal is served featuring the foods that were forbidden during the past few weeks. The main course is often roasted goose, suckling pig or turkey. Finally the dessert table is laid with gingerbread, fruit compotes and kiselj, a sweet soup made of cranberry juice thickened with corn starch.

Christmas celebrations may not be as exuberant as they once were but

ABOVE Father Frost, the Russian equivalent of Santa Claus, and his assistant the Snow Maiden, arrive in central Moscow for the traditional New Year parade.

one of the ancient excitements that remain is the tradition of pouring melted wax into cold water. When the wax hardens the shapes it has made are examined and guesses about what they say about the future are made.

Epiphany

The festival of Epiphany lands on 19 January, and on this day – whatever the weather – some exceptionally hardy Russians take a plunge in their lakes and rivers, which are often so frozen over that chainsaws are needed to cut holes in the ice. This is a symbolic re-enactment of John the Baptist's submersion in the River Jordan. Russian priests bless water on this day, which believers take home and keep through the year, using it as a cure for minor ailments and a beauty treatment for the skin.

Maslenitsa

When Orthodox Christianity was the state religion, the religious holidays were interspersed with strict periods of fasting. The seven weeks of Lent leading up to Easter was a period of restraint, when certain foods were banned, but just before Lent come the feast days of Maslenitsa. Originally an ancient pagan festival to welcome spring, today Maslenitsa is a big public party for both children and adults with theatrical performances, dances and lots of games.

During the week of Maslenitsa, also known as 'Butter Week' the children ride sledges, build snow forts and have snowball fights, while the adults take sleigh rides and drink cognac served from samovars. Outside the cities large bonfires are built and people burn *Tjutjelo*, dolls made with straw symbolizing winter. The week of carnival ends on Shrove Sunday when people ask their friends for forgiveness if they have upset them in any way.

Blinis are the absolute favourite food during Maslenitsa. In Russia it is said that when you eat a blini you get a share of the warmth and the strength from the sun, and during the week of Maslenitsa everyone eats them

BELOW Russian monks enjoy the Easter meal of cake, red caviar and wine.

ABOVE A lavishly spread zakuski table, decorated with the famous Fabergé eggs.

to excess. The blinis are made of wheat floor in a cast iron skillet and as soon as one is ready it is brushed with melted butter and put in a big pile.

The blini should be eaten hot, with a choice of topping. Some people eat them with caviar or smetana while others prefer sugar or jam.

Lent

During Lent the rule for Orthodox Christians is to abstain from meat, animal fat and eggs. Instead they are allowed to eat food such as fresh and pickled vegetable and mushrooms fried in vegetable oil. Over the centuries, much creativity has gone into inventing filling vegetarian dishes: stews, pelmeni, soups, vegetable caviar, pastries with vegetables, mushrooms and fruits. Fish is allowed on some days, when a typical dinner might include fish soup.

Easter

Called *Pascha* in Russian, Easter is the most important festival in the Christian calendar. In Russia it occurs at the same time of year as an old pagan feast marking the end of winter, when the snow thaws and farmers can at last sow their fields with new crops.

Easter is celebrated by Russians wherever they are in the world. One tradition is to select perfect, white eggs to cook and paint. The eggs can also be dyed red by boiling them together with onion skins. These brightly painted eggs are used to brighten up the table and are given as presents to friends and family.

The grand pashka, the Easter cake, dominates the festive table. It is made in a wooden pyramid mould decorated

with religious symbols and the letters 'XB', meaning 'Christ is Risen', stamped in the mould, and contains sweetened soft cheese and raisins. Another favourite Easter cake is kulich, a tall, round confection glazed with sugar and filled with raisins and nuts.

In the old days the pashka, the kulich and the painted eggs were carried to church on Easter Eve. There the priest blessed the Easter food, sprinkling holy water over it out of a silver bowl. It was believed that blessed eggs had magical powers. After the egg had been dipped in a bowl of water, people washed their faces with the same water, guaranteeing good health for the coming year.

A modern Easter party in the 21st century starts with vodka and zakuski (often including chicken liver mousse, marinated mushrooms, and fish salad) and ends with pashka and kulich. In between come many different meat, poultry or fish dishes which have been off the menu for the last seven weeks, such as rabbit in smetana, roast chicken stuffed with sauerkraut and dried fruits, or oven-baked fish. Family and friends are invited to share the Easter feast, and will often drop in throughout the day.

It is common to give eggs as a sign of friendship and appreciation. Every Easter from 1897 Tsar Nikolai II gave bejewelled eggs made by Fabergé in St Petersburg to his wife and his mother. Today these extravagant eggs represent a piece of the Russian Imperial history and the tradition of giving bejewelled eggs has been revived. Many Russians spend money on eggs, either made as a piece of jewellery or as an egg-shaped ornament.

Name day celebrations

All Orthodox Christians are named after a saint, so it is also important to celebrate *Imenini*, or name days (the saint's feast day) in addition to birthdays, and in some ways this celebration is seen as more important since the feast day also has religious significance. Nowadays, people not named after saints also celebrate their name day. Vera, Nadeja, Lubovj and Sofia are all celebrated on the same day – September 10.

On a name day Russians often have a party and eat special treats, but the traditional centrepiece is a large home-made cake, often filled with cottage or curd cheese and raisins, like the Easter pashka. Sometimes there is also a pastry with four corners containing four different fillings, such as apples or berries. At a name day party it is customary that the first three toasts are to the person celebrating. Champagne, home-made liqueurs and tea are served.

Holidays from the Soviet era

During the Soviet era, a number of new holidays were introduced, such as Revolution Day, International Women's Day, Worker's Day, Red Army Day, Navy Day and the Day of Surrender. These new celebrations have largely replaced the religious holidays that are linked to the Orthodox Church. Much of Russia is so far north that the sun barely sets at midsummer, and this gives another good excuse for a two-week celebration known as White Nights in St Petersburg, when there is much eating, drinking and dancing, and very little sleeping.

In the 21st century, Russians take their pick of the holidays on offer and keep Church or state holidays according to their own family tradition. Each holiday is an excuse to enjoy good food and drink, of course, and all Russians like large parties with plenty of zakuski, vodka and champagne.

BELOW Eggs are dyed and elaborately painted as part of Easter celebrations.

BELOW Pashka, the traditional Russian Easter cake, decorated with candied fruit.

BELOW Street parades in traditional costume often mark national holidays.

Zakuski – a mirror of hospitable Russia

These famous appetizers known collectively as zakuski are an old Russian tradition, delicious little dishes of whatever the house has to offer, served as a buffet. The entire country of Russia and all the republics of the former Soviet Union contribute to the dishes included in zakuski and give us a picture of the culinary history of the country.

From a simple appetizer to a laden table

The tradition of zakuski first appeared in the Russian manor houses of past centuries. The guests at a house party arrived in horse-driven carriages at any hour of the day or night, tired from their journey, frozen and hungry. A table with zakuski was always ready in the hallway, so as to greet guests without having to wake up the whole household. On the table, the carafe containing vodka was given the place of honour and during the winter the samovar was constantly sizzling with hot tea. All you had to do was to help yourself to the food and the drink. The zakuski table mirrored the hospitality that Russians are so famous for.

In the beginning, zakuski were an appetizer or a snack, a small matter of some crispy salted cucumbers, smetana (sour cream), a couple of pickles, black bread and a simple fish or meat dish. Gradually the number of dishes on the table increased, and the guests found it harder and harder just to nibble and not fill themselves up with these delicious morsels. Eventually, people were sometimes too full to eat dinner, once it was time to sit down for the main meal of the day.

The way the food was presented as well as the table decorations became very important towards the end of the 1800s, with every beautifully designed dish placed on exquisite platters, with elaborate carved garnishes.

Zakuski and vodka

Russians love to eat and drink, especially in the company of family and friends. Hence they are also very generous and hospitable hosts. Zakuski, which at its minimum is a piece of bread and a salted cucumber, is always served with vodka, often ice cold. If there is a special celebration, champagne is served – at room temperature. There are two important rules: Russians never mix beer and vodka and the hostess should always be served first. But of course zakuski can be enjoyed without alcohol as well, for those who prefer.

Russian celebrations

Any time is the right time to serve zakuski. They are perfect to serve as an appetizer or as a main course. If there is a celebration going on, the zakuski can become especially elaborate and artistic. With many guests arriving, zakuski are perfect, since everything is prepared in advance.

A selection of zakuski

At a celebration the zakuska table can contain as many as ten different dishes, both hot and cold. When the main course is meat, the zakuski are made of fish, and vice versa.

As always in Russia there must be bread on the table, and it should be black sourdough bread. Sometimes sea salt is served in a bowl at the table.

LEFT A fabulous array of condiments and ingredients is spread out in one of the many food stores in the main shopping area of St Petersburg.

ABOVE Russia has many varieties of layered salads, often topped with mayonnaise.

ABOVE Blinis are served with a variety of toppings, often including caviar.

Decorating the table

Topaz-green cucumber, golden pastries, ruby-red cranberries, amber-coloured veal brawn, ivory-white sturgeon and pink salmon – the colours of zakuski shimmer like gems in the candlelight. To reflect this, the zakuski table should always be beautifully laid out. The first thing to consider is the tablecloth. Choose a large cloth, preferably with lace trimmings, then decorate the table with flowers and one or two candelabra. The light from the candles should be reflected in beautiful glass or crystal bowls and silver platters. The chilled vodka is put out in its original bottle with small glasses to drink it from. There should also be a couple of bottles of champagne or Russian sparkling wine on the table.

Bread and salt (chleb and solj) are ever present on the Russian table, and *chlebosoljstvo* is the Russian word for hospitality. Freshly boiled potatoes, often mixed with finely chopped dill, melted butter or smetana, are another important element.

Salted herring is served with golden mustard sauce or with smetana and chopped leek for Herring à la Russe.

You can also serve the herring covered with finely chopped hard-boiled eggs and vegetables. This variation is called sjuba, meaning 'fur' – herring in a fur coat. Many dishes include smoked fish. There should also be some sort of caviar on the table. Often the famous Salat Olivje is included, and there will be some kind of 'poor man's caviar' made of vegetables.

Pickles are always a part of the zakuski table. Sauerkraut should be there, of course, but also marinated tomatoes and pickled mushrooms.

How to eat zakuski

The meal is started by the host greeting everybody with a welcome and a toast – 'za zdorovie!' (good health). Then everybody helps themselves to the delicacies on the table.

To start with, dip the salted cucumber in smetana and honey. It is a simple but elegant dish that goes well with the first glass of ice-cold vodka. Then move on to the herring and the caviar and add some of the newly boiled potatoes with their aroma of dill. After the fish, it is time to concentrate on the meat and vegetables and the different pickles.

If there is vodka or champagne to go with the zakuski there will most probably be a lot of toasting. The toasts will begin for something special that is worth celebrating, but if there is a lack of real reasons the toast can be for almost anything. A toast for peace, understanding and absent friends is always a good idea. Maybe this constant toasting is a way to make sure that nobody stays sober. Eating zakuski is a social affair, just as much about having fun together as it is about the food and drink.

BELOW Russians love mushrooms, and preserve them for eating through winter.

Classic ingredients

Russia is like a giant pantry, full of all that the good earth yields from rivers and lakes, forests and meadows. For centuries the rural population survived exclusively on locally grown produce, until gradually communications became better and even perishable goods could be transported from one end of the country to the other by road and rail.

Russia offers all weathers, from scorching heat in the summer to freezing cold in the winter. The genuine Russian cuisine, however, has its roots in Central Russia where the winters are long but the summers pleasantly warm. Here the harvests of hops, rye, oats and wheat and of vegetables and fruits are abundant. The woods are full of seasonal harvests of berries, mushrooms and herbs. The rivers and the lakes yield freshwater fish like carp, bream, pike-perch and pike while the green pastures support both meat and milk production.

Russians are very proud of their fertile land, and love to grow the staple ingredients themselves. Many people have a little patch of land on which they grow vegetables, with maybe a chicken or two for eggs and meat. These supplies were essential in the Soviet era, when there was not much available in the store.

ABOVE Hops.

Grains

No Russian meal, at any time of day, would be complete without some rye or wheat bread. The meal is simply not ready to serve until the bread has been put out. Other grains such as pearl barley, buckwheat and rice are also popular, and add substance to many a soup or stew when there is not much meat to be had.

Rye

When grains first began to be grown on a large scale, Russians discovered that rye yields more dependable harvests than the more delicate wheat, and with rye sourdough you could make bread that stayed fresh for a long time. Black (rye) bread is still the most popular kind of bread in Russia.

Wheat and buckwheat

Nowadays bread is also made with wheat flour. Wheat flour is used for pastry, and for pelmeni as well, the Russian pasta dumplings that rather resemble ravioli, little pockets of pasta with a tasty filling.

Buckwheat flour is slightly grey in colour and free of gluten, so it is ideal for special diets. It has more taste than ordinary white flour and is sometimes mixed with wheat flour to make blinis.

Vegetables

The fertility of the soil in most parts of Russia and the culture of maintaining a kitchen garden have both led to an emphasis on vegetables of all kinds in Russian cuisine.

Cabbage

This is a real staple food of Russia, and indeed of most European and Asian countries. It is a nutritious vegetable

LEFT Pearl barley. RIGHT White cabbage.

ABOVE Swede.

that grows through the winter and keeps well. Cabbage soup is a peasant dish that can contain a whole variety of ingredients apart from the cabbage, depending on what is available. The large outer leaves of cabbage are used for cabbage rolls, stuffed with a tasty mixture of meat or fish, and the inner leaves are also popular in a raw salad.

Sauerkraut

This preserved cabbage can be kept for up to seven months and has played an important role for the peasant population during the long cold winters. The technique is to slice the cabbage finely, season it with salt and then let it mature in an oak barrel or, if made at home, in a jar. Nowadays sauerkraut is usually bought ready prepared in markets, it is also widely available in cans. Sauerkraut is often served with sausages or poultry.

Potatoes

These versatile vegetables were introduced to Russia by Peter the Great more than 250 years ago. Potatoes are ubiquitous in Russian cooking, whether as a separate vegetable accompaniment, in a stew, or cooked

and cooled as part of a salad. Cold boiled potatoes with a sour cream dressing and plenty of dill are a favourite part of the zakuski table.

Beetroot

The immensely popular beetroot (beet) was first cultivated in Ukraine as far back as the 11th century. Beets are not only made into a rich satisfying soup with sour cream (borscht); they are an essential part of many salads, and form the basis of a topping for blinis known as beetroot caviar.

Other root vegetables

Russians are very keen on root vegetables. Swede, black radish, carrots, onions and turnips were the most common roots in the old days and are still used today. Turnips, however, are now often substituted for potatoes.

Cooking with sauerkraut
Gentle simmering in a stew is a simple and delicious way to use sauerkraut. These casseroles become even tastier when left to stew overnight. As with all kinds of slow home cooking, the results vary according to the taste of the cook and the ingredients that happen to be available. Sauerkraut can also be fried with onions and then cooked in wine or water. The really extravagant Russian cooks his sauerkraut in champagne.

ABOVE Salted cucumber.

Salted cucumber

Russians love salted cucumbers. They are made by preserving them with herbs and maybe garlic or horseradish. The traditional salted cucumbers are made by preserving them in layers with salt, spices and oak or cherry tree leaves in large oak barrels. Salted cucumbers, whether home-made or ready bought, have many uses in Russian cuisine. They can be eaten just as they are with honey or smetana as a zakuski, added to soups such as soljanka or rassoljnik, or even made into hot and cold sauces.

Mushrooms

These earthy, rich vegetables are an integral part of many Russian recipes. Mushrooms are easily found growing in the forests and woods of the countryside, and many families still go mushroom picking today. The best-loved mushrooms in Russia are ceps, or porcini. They are delicious with most food, and of all wild mushrooms they are the easiest to dry, making them available all year round. Fresh and preserved mushrooms are used in appetizers, in soups, in sauces for vegetable and meat dishes and in fillings for pies and pasties.

ABOVE Cottage cheese.

ABOVE Eggs.

Dairy products

Cow's milk is not much used in Russia, but other products from the dairy cow are extremely popular. Yogurt, cottage cheese and curd (farmer's) cheese all keep longer than fresh milk, a practical proposition in both town and country. Cottage or curd cheese is spread on sandwiches and also mixed with vegetables and flour or grains. It can be blended with sugar or honey and spices as part of the filling for Easter cakes or blinis.

Smetana, a sharp, thick sour cream is a very important ingredient in Russian cuisine. It is frequently added as a thickener in soups and sauces – in salads such as potato salad – and as a topping for all sorts of food, such as blinis. Its distinctive taste blends well in both savoury and sweet dishes.

Eggs

'Round as an egg' was an old Russian saying to describe a beautiful young girl. This was a great compliment, as eggs were really precious to the Russians. They are indispensable in pelmeni (Russian pasta dumplings) and lapsha, sweet cakes, omelettes and pancakes. Egg dishes are fast to cook and very nutritious. A perfect, cheap Russian dinner will consist of a couple of fried eggs, a piece of bread and two or three fried sausages.

Meat, poultry and game

Russians love meat and it often forms the main course for lunch or supper, and always for larger celebratory meals. On these important occasions the meat is often prepared whole, and roasted suckling pig, chicken or goose are characteristic dishes for Easter or New Year feasts. The lesser cuts need tenderizing, and this is achieved by simmering on a low heat for a long time in a covered pot. Most Russian meat dishes blend well with grains, mushrooms and other vegetables.

Beef, pork and lamb

One of the most well-known Russian dishes is Beef Stroganoff, a rich mixture of best-quality beef and sour cream. Lesser cuts of beef and pork are often mixed together, minced (ground) and formed into burgers with buckwheat and onion, and the sweeter taste of lamb blends well with aubergines (eggplants) and tomatoes in tasty baked casseroles.

Poultry

Chicken and goose dishes are very popular, particularly as they were widely available in the countryside when the more expensive beef and lamb were hard to find. Chicken in Walnut Sauce is a traditional dish from Georgia, where walnut trees thrive in the relatively warm climate. The famous Chicken Kiev from Ukraine has been adopted by cooks throughout the world.

Game

Animals such as rabbit, bear, deer and hare are still hunted in the forests of rural Russia. These strong-tasting meats are generally cooked in the oven or simmered in a sauce to tenderize them and make the most of the fragrant gravy.

Fish

Russian cuisine offers a wide variety of both cold and hot fish dishes. The most popular way to prepare the best, freshest fish is to simply fry it. To keep in the juices and flavour it is coated with breadcrumbs or flour and then fried in a flavourless oil such as rapeseed (canola) or sunflower.

BELOW Cod steak.

Sea fish

Larger white fish such as flounder, sole or halibut can be baked whole with smetana in the oven, or chopped into pieces to be gently simmered in an alcoholic sauce with vodka or wine.

Freshwater fish

The huge lakes and rivers of Russia contain many different varieties of freshwater fish. Russian recipes really make the most of these, with plenty of ideas for using perch, pike and carp, particularly as main courses when meat is off the menu, for example during Lent. These rather solid fish really benefit from being marinated in a spicy dressing before cooking.

Caviar

The roe from cod or pike used to be the single most important dish on the table. Over time sturgeon caviar became the most popular, and in the 1800s a well-to-do Russian family might present a bowl containing 20 kilos of caviar on their zakuski table, with a large silver spoon so that their guests could help themselves to this salty treat. In the West, caviar has come to represent utter luxury. Today

BELOW Caviar.

ABOVE Raisins.

wild sturgeon are nearly extinct and real, original Russian caviar is more expensive than ever. However, a lesser quality black sturgeon roe can still be found at a lower price.

Spices and flavourings

In addition to salt and pepper, the staple flavourings of most Russian dishes, other recipes are enlivened by a whole range of herbs, spices and other flavourings grown in rural Russia and the surrounding countries on its borders for centuries.

Herbs

Dill and parsley are the most commonly used herbs in Russian cooking. They blend particularly well with many vegetables, and are especially used in potato dishes.

Horseradish

Russian cuisine is generally quite mild and if you want to add a little extra zing it often will be in the form of shredded fresh horseradish.

Poppy seeds

In common with most Eastern countries, fragrant poppy seeds are a favourite in Russia, often used as a topping to be sprinkled over sweet dishes and bread.

Garlic

Caucasian and Uzbekistan cooks use a lot of garlic, giving these regional recipes a distinctively aromatic flavour.

Berries

Russians are very diligent at finding and preserving what nature provides, and berry picking with the family is one of their great pleasures in the autumn.

Russians love the sour taste of cranberries, which are used to make the drink mors. Other types of berries, such as lingonberries, redcurrants, blueberries and raspberries are used in cakes and desserts and for making jam and preserves.

Honey

In the past honey was used as a preservative as well as a sweetener. Drinks such as sbitenj and medok have honey as their main ingredient. These drinks are served in restaurants and at home. Kvass, a kind of a light beer, perfect for quenching the thirst in the summer, is also sweetened with honey.

BELOW Cranberries.

SOUPS

Fish Soup with Salted Cucumber
and Capers

Beetroot Soup

Ukrainian Borscht

Chicken Noodle Soup

Georgian Meat Soup

Fresh Cabbage Soup

Veal Kidney and Cucumber Soup

Cold Beetroot Soup

Cold Kvass Soup

Hearty and filling

Russians have a passion for their soups, both hot and cold. Hot, filling soups are served during the harsh winter months, when there is a special need for sustaining food that warms from the inside out. Borscht, the famous beet soup with its splendid ruby-red colour, is perhaps the best-known hot Russian soup, but cabbage soup (sjchi) is also very popular. Even Catherine the Great enjoyed sjchi and developed a ritual around it. Her guests would gather in the so-called Diamond Room where a table would be laid out with serving bowls of purest gold, each of them covered in a linen cloth, containing cabbage soup. When the servant called out 'Lids!' – the lids were lifted simultanously from the bowls at which moment Catherine made her appearance. The freezing temperatures of Russian winters last longer than the warm summer days, so there are fewer recipes for cold soups. Two favourites are okroshka, a soup made with kvass, a light beer, and svekoljnik, which is made from beetroot. Both are popular as a refreshing appetizer in the summer heat.

Fish Soup with Salted Cucumber and Capers
Rybnaja Soljanka

This fish soup is considered to be the queen of Russian soups. Its lovely, rich flavour is accentuated by the salty additions of Salted Cucumbers, capers and olives. If you can find sturgeon, use it instead of the halibut and turbot suggested in the recipe. If you make your own fish stock then the recipe will be even more special.

Serves 4

2 onions
2–3 carrots
1 parsnip
200g/7oz Salted Cucumbers
30–45ml/2–3 tbsp rapeseed (canola) oil
15ml/1 tbsp tomato purée (paste)
1 bay leaf
4–5 black peppercorns
1 litre/1¾ pints/4 cups home-made or
    good quality fish stock
400–500g/14oz–1¼lb salmon, halibut and
    turbot fillets, skinned
8 green olives
8 black olives
30ml/2 tbsp capers plus 5ml/1 tsp juice
    from the jar
4 thin lemon slices
60ml/4 tbsp smetana or crème fraîche
45ml/3 tbsp chopped fresh dill, to garnish

1 Finely chop the onions. Dice the carrots, parsnip and finely dice the cucumbers. Heat the oil in a large pan, add the onions and fry over a medium heat for 2–3 minutes, until softened. Add the carrots and parsnip and fry over a medium heat, stirring all the time, for 5 minutes.

2 Add the cucumbers, tomato purée, bay leaf and peppercorns to the pan and fry for a further 2–3 minutes. Add half of the stock, cover and bring to the boil. Reduce the heat and simmer for 10 minutes.

3 Meanwhile, cut the fish into 2cm/¾in cubes. Add the remaining stock, green and black olives, the capers and the caper juice to the pan. Return to the boil and add the fish cubes. Reduce the heat and simmer for 5 minutes, until the fish is just tender, being careful not to overcook the fish.

4 To serve, spoon the soup into warmed bowls, add a slice of lemon, a spoonful of smetana or crème fraîche and garnish with chopped dill.

VARIATION
Soups that use Salted Cucumbers as an ingredient are often called soljanka. There are also soljankas that contain cooked meat. Just substitute the fish for 300–400g/11–14oz mixed boiled beef, ham and sausages.

Energy 389kcal/1613kJ; Protein 24.5g; Carbohydrate 9.1g, of which sugars 7.2g; Fat 28.5g, of which saturates 7.7g; Cholesterol 73mg; Calcium 74mg; Fibre 3.1g; Sodium 361mg.

Beetroot Soup
Borstj

This famous soup is the centre and highlight of the Russian meal. There are many versions of the recipe, which are often passed on in the family, and the young, who gladly follow the advice and tips of their grandmothers, are taught to cook it from a very early age. The secret behind a good borsht is the home-made stock and the high quality of the root vegetables that are used.

Serves 4–6

5–6 beetroots (beets), total weight 500g/1¼lb
3 carrots, total weight 250g/9oz
1 cabbage wedge, total weight 300g/11oz
3 potatoes
2 onions
45ml/3 tbsp tomato purée (paste)
15ml/1 tbsp sugar
5ml/1 tsp salt
60–90ml/4–6 tbsp smetana or crème fraîche
chopped fresh dill, to garnish
4–6 lemon wedges, to serve

For the stock

1kg/2¼lb beef on the bone
2 litres/3½ pints/8 cups water
1 carrot
1 parsnip
1 piece celeriac
1 onion
2 bay leaves
4–5 black peppercorns
2–3 fresh parsley stalks
5ml/1 tsp salt

1 To make the stock, put the beef and bones in a large pan, add the water and bring to the boil. Lower the heat and simmer for 10 minutes, skimming the surface of any residue that rises to the top.

2 Add the carrot, parsnip, celeriac, onion, bay leaves, peppercorns, parsley and salt to the pan. Cover and simmer gently for 1 hour. Remove the vegetables and seasonings from the pan and discard them. Remove the meat from the pan and cut into small chunks.

3 To make the soup, add the beetroots and carrots to the pan, bring to the boil then simmer for about 40 minutes, until the vegetables are tender. Remove the beetroots and carrots from the pan and leave to cool.

4 Meanwhile, thinly slice the cabbage and onions and dice the potatoes. Add to the pan, bring the stock back to the boil then simmer for 15–20 minutes.

5 Coarsely grate the cooled beetroots and carrots. When the cabbage, onions and potatoes are tender, add the beetroot and carrot to the soup with the tomato purée, sugar and salt. Add the meat. Simmer for a further 10 minutes.

6 To serve, pour the soup into warmed bowls. Top each serving with 2–3 pieces of meat, 15ml/1 tbsp smetana or crème fraîche and chopped dill to garnish. Accompany with a lemon wedge.

COOK'S TIP
It is a good idea to make double the quantity of this recipe and freeze what you don't need. The soup is easy to heat up for a quick but delicious meal.

Energy 127kcal/535kJ; Protein 4g; Carbohydrate 20.2g, of which sugars 17.7g; Fat 4g, of which saturates 2.3g; Cholesterol 9mg; Calcium 60mg; Fibre 5g; Sodium 143mg.

Serves 4
4–5 medium beetroots (beets)
1 carrot
1 small piece celeriac
1 small onion
1 small wedge cabbage
2 potatoes
1 red (bell) pepper
juice of ½ lemon
300g/11oz cooked boiled beef
60–75ml/4–5 tbsp rapeseed (canola) oil
30ml/2 tbsp tomato purée (paste)
1.5 litres/2½ pints/6¼ cups beef stock
3–4 garlic cloves
50g/2oz salo or lardo
15ml/1 tbsp sugar
salt
bread rolls, to serve

Ukrainian Borscht
Ukrainskij Borstj

This borscht is flavoured with salo, salted pig's lard, but
you can also use Italian lardo. This Italian cured pork fat,
eaten as an antipasto, is classified as a cold meat.

1 Coarsely grate the beetroots, carrot
and celeriac. Chop the onion and
finely slice the cabbage.

2 Peel and cut the potatoes into
wedges. Finely slice the pepper,
discarding the core and seeds.
Squeeze the juice from the lemon,
and cut the beef into small chunks.

3 Heat the oil in a large frying pan.
Add the grated beetroots, carrot and
celeriac, the onion and cabbage then
stir-fry for 10 minutes, until softened.

4 Add the potatoes, tomato purée and
half of the stock to the pan. Bring to
the boil then reduce the heat and
simmer for 15 minutes. Add the
remaining stock and the pepper and
simmer for a further 5–10 minutes,
until all the vegetables are tender.

5 Meanwhile, chop the garlic. Put in a
mortar with the salo or lardo and
grind together with a pestle.

6 Add the meat to the soup, bring to
the boil, then turn off the heat. Stir
in the lemon juice, sugar and garlic
mixture, and season to taste. Serve
with warmed bread rolls.

Energy 483kcal/2015kJ; Protein 22.4g; Carbohydrate 36.5g, of which sugars 20.8g; Fat 28.4g, of which saturates 9g; Cholesterol 55mg; Calcium 75mg; Fibre 5.7g; Sodium 169mg.

Serves 4

1 small chicken
1.5 litres/2½ pints/6¼ cups water
1 onion, cut into wedges
1 carrot, peeled and sliced
1 parsnip, peeled and sliced
1 leek, white parts only, cut into chunks
5ml/1 tsp salt
45ml/3 tbsp finely chopped parsley,
   to garnish
60ml/4 tbsp smetana or crème fraîche,
   to serve

For the noodles

150g/5oz/1¼ cups plain white (all-
   purpose) flour
1 egg
30–45ml/2–3 tbsp cold water
1.5ml/¼ tsp salt

Chicken Noodle Soup
Lapsha

The Russians are masters at making a good stock and this recipe is a good example. It is said that the stock should be translucent and as clear as a teardrop.

COOK'S TIP
Only half the noodles are required for this recipe. Keep the remaining noodles in an airtight container for up to a week in the refrigerator, or freeze. Substitute ready-made noodles if you are short of time.

1 Put the chicken in a large pan, add the water and bring to the boil. Reduce the heat and simmer for 5 minutes. Skim the surface. Add the onion, carrot, parsnip, leek and salt to the pan, cover and simmer over a low-medium heat for 45 minutes, or until the chicken is tender.

2 Using a slotted spoon, remove the vegetables from the pan and discard. Transfer the chicken to a plate, and leave to cool. Pass the stock through a sieve (strainer) and pour back into the pan. When the chicken is cool, cut into bitesize pieces.

3 To make the noodles, put the flour, egg, water and salt in a food processor and blend to a smooth dough. Put on a floured surface and knead for 2–3 minutes. Wrap in clear film (plastic wrap) and leave to rest in the refrigerator for 30 minutes.

4 Divide the dough into four even pieces. Using a rolling pin or pasta machine, roll out one piece at a time until very thin, and then cut into 5–6cm/2–2½in strips. Leave the strips to dry for 5 minutes. Place a few strips on top of each other and shred them diagonally into very thin strips. Toss in flour and allow them to dry.

5 To serve the soup, put the chicken pieces into four individual serving bowls. Bring the stock to the boil, add half the noodles and cook for 5 minutes. Pour into the soup bowls, garnish with chopped parsley and accompany with smetana or crème fraîche.

Energy 427kcal/1805kJ; Protein 54.5g; Carbohydrate 40.2g, of which sugars 7.8g; Fat 6.4g, of which saturates 1.7g; Cholesterol 152mg; Calcium 76mg; Fibre 5.3g; Sodium 237mg.

Serves 4

1.2kg/2½lb chunky pieces breast or
  shoulder lamb, on the bone
1.5 litres/2½ pints/6¼ cups water
3 large onions
½ mild chilli
5 garlic cloves
2 tomatoes
45–60ml/4–5 tbsp olive oil
15ml/1 tbsp tomato purée (paste)
45–60ml/4–5 tbsp long grain rice
45–60ml/4–5 tbsp chopped fresh parsley
salt
45ml/3 tbsp chopped fresh coriander
  (cilantro), to garnish
60ml/4 tbsp Plum Sauce (see recipe for
  Kebabs with Plum Sauce), to serve

VARIATION
Instead of serving the soup with Plum
Sauce, try adding 3–4 chopped fresh
plums to the rice.

Georgian Meat Soup Harcho

With its lovely aroma of garlic, and its smooth, creamy
texture, this is the king of soups in Georgia. It is one of
the most popular dishes served in Russian restaurants
and is served on both festive occasions and weekdays.

1 Put the meat in a large pan, add the
water and bring to the boil. Reduce
the heat and simmer for 5 minutes.
Skim the surface, cover with a lid and
simmer for 50–60 minutes, until the
meat is just tender.

2 Meanwhile, roughly chop the
onions. Remove the seeds from the
chilli. Finely chop the garlic. Slice the
tomatoes into wedges.

3 Heat the oil in a large frying pan.
Add the onions and fry for about
5 minutes, until golden brown. Add
the tomato purée and the tomatoes
and fry, stirring all the time, for a
further 1 minute.

4 Add the onion mixture, rice,
parsley, chilli and garlic to the meat.
Season with salt to taste and cook for
a further 20–25 minutes.

5 To serve, divide the meat between
four soup bowls, pour the soup on
top, and sprinkle with chopped
coriander to garnish. Accompany the
soup with the Plum Sauce.

Energy 433kcal/1801kJ; Protein 27.6g; Carbohydrate 24g, of which sugars 12g; Fat 25.5g, of which saturates 8.1g; Cholesterol 95mg; Calcium 72mg; Fibre 2.6g; Sodium 369mg.

Fresh Cabbage Soup
Svegii Stjii

Soups play an important part in Russian cuisine and this vegetarian soup is one of the most popular everyday soups. Every housewife has her own recipe and the variations and adaptations are endless.

Serves 4

40g/1½oz/3 tbsp butter
1 onion, sliced
1 head white cabbage, total weight 750g/1lb 10oz, shredded
1 carrot, shredded or grated
1 piece celeriac, total weight 50g/2oz, shredded and grated
2 bay leaves
5 black peppercorns
1.5 litres/2½ pints/6¼ cups vegetable stock
5 new potatoes, diced
15ml/1 tbsp sunflower oil
1 (bell) pepper, cored and sliced
2 tomatoes, chopped
salt and ground black pepper
45ml/3 tbsp chopped fresh dill, to garnish
smetana or crème fraîche and rye bread, to serve

1 Melt the butter in a large pan over a medium heat. Add the onion and cook, stirring frequently, for 3 minutes, until softened but not browned. Add the cabbage, carrot and celeriac and cook for 3 minutes.

2 Add the bay leaves, peppercorns and 200ml/7fl oz/scant 1 cup of stock. Bring to the boil then reduce the heat, cover and simmer for 15 minutes, stirring occasionally.

3 Add the remaining stock and the potatoes and simmer for further 10 minutes until the potatoes are soft.

4 Meanwhile, heat the oil in a small frying pan over medium heat. Add the pepper and tomatoes and fry for 2–3 minutes, until softened. Transfer the pepper and tomatoes to the soup and simmer for 5 minutes. Season with salt and pepper to taste.

5 Spoon the soup into bowls, and sprinkle with the chopped dill. Top with smetana or crème fraîche and accompany with rye bread.

Energy 273kcal/1141kJ; Protein 6g; Carbohydrate 36.7g, of which sugars 17.4g; Fat 12.2g, of which saturates 5.8g; Cholesterol 21mg; Calcium 122mg; Fibre 7.2g; Sodium 106mg.

Veal Kidney and Cucumber Soup
Rassoljnik s Lezjenom

Many Russians prefer this soup to be as thick as porridge (kasha) but a thinner consistency may be more to your taste. It is important not boil the soup after the Lezjen sauce has been added, otherwise it may curdle.

Serves 4

1.5 litres/2½ pints/6¼ cups home-made or good quality beef stock
50g/2oz/generous ¼ cup pearl barley
4–5 potatoes
1 onion
1 small leek
2 carrots
50g/2oz celeriac
3–4 Salted Cucumbers plus 30ml–45ml/2–3 tbsp juice from the jar
600g/1lb 6oz calf's kidney
45ml/3 tbsp rapeseed (canola) oil
2 bay leaves
5 black peppercorns
2 allspice berries
25g/1oz chopped fresh dill or 50g/2oz chopped fresh parsley

For the Lezjen sauce

15g/½oz/1 tbsp butter
1 egg yolk
75ml/5 tbsp double (heavy) cream

COOK'S TIP
Do not boil the soup after the sauce has been added as it might curdle.

VARIATION
As a quick alternative to making the Lezjen Sauce, you can also top the soup with smetana or crème fraîche.

1 Heat half of the stock in a large pan. Add the barley and cook for 35–50 minutes until soft. Meanwhile, cut the potatoes into small wedges and add to the pan for the last 10 minutes of cooking.

2 Meanwhile, chop the onion, slice the leek, finely slice the carrots and celeriac, and dice the pickled cucumbers. Cut the calf's kidney into small chunks.

3 Heat the oil in a large frying pan. Add the onion, leek, carrots and celeriac and fry over a medium heat, stirring occasionally, for about 10 minutes, until softened.

4 Add the Salted Cucumbers, bay leaves, peppercorns and allspice to the pan, and fry for a further 1–2 minutes, stirring all the time.

5 Add the vegetable and cucumber mixture to the pan together with the cooked barley and potatoes. Add the kidney and the remaining stock and simmer for 20 minutes.

6 Just before serving, make the sauce. Melt the butter in a pan.

7 Remove the pan from the heat and mix in the egg yolk and cream. Alternatively, make the sauce in advance and keep warm in a bowl, uncovered, standing over a pan of hot water at a maximum of 55ºC/130ºF, until ready to serve.

8 Add the dill or parsley to the soup and season with the Salted Cucumber juice, according to taste. Bring the soup back to the boil, stirring all the time. Remove from the heat and serve immediately, topped with the sauce.

Energy 515kcal/2152kJ; Protein 29.7g; Carbohydrate 38.5g, of which sugars 8.6g; Fat 27.9g, of which saturates 11.4g; Cholesterol 684mg; Calcium 107mg; Fibre 4.7g; Sodium 340mg.

Serves 4

800g/1¾lb small raw beetroots (beets)
1.2 litres/2 pints/5 cups water
4 medium potatoes
3 eggs
2–3 cucumbers, total weight 300g/11oz
1 bunch spring onions (scallions)
15ml/1 tbsp mustard
60ml/4 tbsp smetana or crème fraîche
15–30ml/1–2 tbsp fresh lemon juice
5–15ml/2–3 tsp sugar
salt
60–75ml/4–5 tbsp finely chopped fresh
   dill, to garnish

COOK'S TIP

This soup can be prepared in advance up to step 3 until ready to serve.

Cold Beetroot Soup
Svekoljnik

All year around, soup is the heart of every Russian meal. In the summer the soups are often served chilled, as in this recipe, to be enjoyed in the summer heat.

1 Put the beetroot in a pan, add the water and 5ml/1 tsp salt and bring to the boil. Boil for about 50 minutes, until soft. Leave to cool in the stock.

2 Put the potatoes in a pan of salted water. Bring to the boil and cook for 20 minutes, until soft. Drain.

3 Put the eggs in a pan, cover with cold water and bring to the boil. Reduce the heat, and simmer for 10 minutes. Drain and put under cold running water. Remove the shells and chop the eggs.

4 When the beetroots are cold, pour the beetroot stock into a jug (pitcher) or bowl and put in the refrigerator. Remove the skin from the beetroots, and coarsely grate or cut into thin strips. Dice the cold potatoes. Cut the cucumbers into strips and finely chop the spring onions.

5 Put the beetroots in a soup tureen or large serving bowl. Add the potatoes, cucumbers, eggs, spring onions and the mustard and mix.

6 To serve, pour the beetroot stock over the beetroots in the serving bowl, add the smetana or crème fraîche and mix gently together. Season with the lemon juice, sugar and salt to taste. Sprinkle the chopped dill on top to garnish.

Energy 215kcal/908kJ; Protein 11.8g; Carbohydrate 28.9g, of which sugars 19.9g; Fat 6.8g, of which saturates 2.3g; Cholesterol 147mg; Calcium 122mg; Fibre 6.3g; Sodium 311mg.

Serves 4

2 eggs
15ml/1 tbsp mustard
100ml/3½fl oz/scant ½ cup smetana
  or crème fraîche plus 60ml/4 tbsp,
  to serve
1 litre/1¾ pints/4 cups kvass or
  buttermilk (see Cook's tip)
250g/9oz cooked meat, such as
  unsmoked ham or roast pork, or
  cooked sausages
1 cucumber, total weight 250g/9oz
1 bunch spring onions (scallions)
15ml/1 tbsp sugar
45ml/3 tbsp finely chopped fresh dill
salt

Cold Kvass Soup
Okroshka

Kvass is a fermented drink, low in alcohol, which is made from wheat. It can also be used as a basis for this soup, known as okroshka. This soup is very easy to make and is perfect on a lazy summer day. Chilled, tasty okroshka will cool you even on the hottest day.

1 Put the eggs in a pan, cover with cold water and bring to the boil. Reduce the heat and simmer for 10 minutes. Drain and put under cold running water. Shell the eggs and separate the yolks from the whites.

2 Put the egg yolks in a soup tureen or bowl and mash until smooth. Add the mustard and the 100ml/3½fl oz/ scant ½ cup smetana or crème fraîche and mix together. Slowly mix in the kvass or buttermilk.

3 Chop the egg whites. Dice the meat or sausages. Finely slice the cucumber and spring onions. Add the meat, cucumber, spring onions, and egg whites to the egg yolk mixture and mix together. Add the sugar and dill and season with salt to taste.

4 To serve, pour the soup into soup bowls and top with the remaining smetana or crème fraîche.

VARIATION
If you cannot find kvass, a sweet, wheat-based drink, buttermilk will give a different but equally good flavour.

Energy 353kcal/1473kJ; Protein 27.6g; Carbohydrate 17.6g, of which sugars 17.3g; Fat 19.8g, of which saturates 10.3g; Cholesterol 169mg; Calcium 363mg; Fibre 0.8g; Sodium 305mg.

APPETIZERS

Chopped Herring Salad

Cold Cod Salad

Layered Herring Salad

Crab Salad

Russian Pancakes

Veal Brawn

Chicken Liver Pâté

Russian Salad

Salted Cucumbers

Marinated Mushrooms

Beetroot Caviar

Tempting little dishes

The tasty appetizers, known in Russia as zakuski, are served at the beginning of most Russian meals. The only difference between a weekday supper and a large celebration dinner is in the number of dishes and the way they are presented. For an everyday meal zakuski are served as an appetizer and should not be too filling. They are only meant to wake up your taste buds and your appetite, and for this reason many of them contain a salty fish or shellfish, such as herring or crab. 'The best of the Russian zakuski, if you want to know, is the herring,' stated the Russian author Chekhov. These delicate dishes are also ideal for a light lunch or supper in their own right. At parties zakuski are much more elaborate. They can consist of ten or more dishes, both hot and cold. Cooks are careful to contrast the zakuski with the main course – when the main dish consists of meat or poultry, the zakuski will be based on fish, and vice versa. Mushrooms, aubergines (eggplants) and beetroot (beets) are the ideal accompaniment as salads.

Serves 6
250g/9oz salted or pickled herring fillets
2 eggs
45ml/3 tbsp rapeseed (canola) oil
1 onion, finely chopped
1 Granny Smith apple
40g/1½oz/3 tbsp butter, at
   room temperature
1–2 spring onions (scallions), to garnish

Chopped Herring Salad
Forshmak Seljdj Rubleniaja

Although the ingredients for this dish are simple, it is usually served at festive occasions.
The herring fillets must be soaked overnight, so allow time to do this. You can buy ready-
made forshmak in Russian delicatessens. It is delicious served with ice cold vodka.

1 If using salted herrings, soak the fillets in cold water overnight. The next day, rinse the herring fillets under running water and then drain.

2 Put the eggs in a pan, cover with cold water and bring to the boil. Reduce the heat and simmer for 10 minutes. Meanwhile, heat the oil in a frying pan, add the chopped onion and fry for about 5 minutes, until softened but not browned. Set aside.

3 When the eggs are cooked, drain and put under cold running water. Remove the shell and separate the yolks from the whites.

4 Peel, core and chop the apple and put in a food processor. Add the salted or pickled herring fillets, egg yolks and the butter and process to a paste. Transfer to a bowl and mix in the fried onion.

5 Finely chop the reserved egg whites and finely slice the spring onions. Put the salad on a serving plate and serve garnished with the chopped egg whites and spring onions.

Energy 212kcal/875kJ; Protein 7.6g; Carbohydrate 3.2g, of which sugars 2.8g; Fat 18.9g, of which saturates 4.6g; Cholesterol 97mg; Calcium 32mg; Fibre 0.3g; Sodium 223mg.

Serves 6-8

600g/1lb 6oz cod fillets, skinned
5ml/1 tsp salt
4-5 black peppercorns
1 bay leaf
200ml/7fl oz/scant 1 cup rapeseed
  (canola) oil
3 large onions, diced
3 large carrots, grated
45ml/3 tbsp water
200g/7oz/scant 1 cup mayonnaise

Cold Cod Salad
Salat iz Treski pod Sjuboj

This salad, with its golden top, was created during the Soviet era when there was a shortage of food. If nothing else, cod, carrots and onions were always to be found in the supermarket 'Gastronom'. The salad is best if chilled overnight, so make it in advance.

1 Put the cod fillets in a pan and add water to just cover. Add the salt, peppercorns and bay leaf, bring to the boil then reduce the heat and simmer for 5-10 minutes. Drain and leave to cool.

2 Heat half of the oil in a large frying pan. Add the onions and fry, stirring, until golden brown. Remove from the pan and set aside to cool.

3 Heat the remaining oil in the frying pan, add the grated carrots and fry over medium heat, stirring, for 10 minutes. Add the water and continue cooking for 5-10 minutes, until the water has evaporated. Set aside.

4 Divide the cooled fish into small chunks, removing all bones, and spread on a large serving dish. Cover the fish with the onions and spread the carrots on top. Cover with mayonnaise. Chill for 2-3 hours or overnight before serving.

VARIATION
As an alternative, you can substitute the cod with perch, pike or other white fish.

Energy 528kcal/2179kJ; Protein 15.3g; Carbohydrate 9.5g, of which sugars 7.5g; Fat 47.9g, of which saturates 6.6g; Cholesterol 63mg; Calcium 38mg; Fibre 2g; Sodium 225mg.

Layered Herring Salad
Forshmak, Seljdj Rublennaja

This salad looks like a cake, and is internationally called Herring à la Russe. The cover under which the herrings dwell is made from several layers of vegetables and mayonnaise, and is always topped with grated hard-boiled eggs. Every Russian cook has their own recipe that they are unwilling to divulge. This herring dish is served both on the zakuski table and as a main course. Many Russians would also gladly eat what is left for breakfast.

Serves 8 as an appetizer,
  4 as a main course
250g/9oz salted herring fillets
3 carrots, total weight 250g/9oz
4 eggs
1 small red onion
200g/7oz/scant 1 cup mayonnaise
5–6 cooked beetroots (beets), total weight
  300g/11oz
2 Granny Smith apples
45ml/3 tbsp chopped fresh dill

VARIATION
Make this dish with pickled beetroot for an added tang of vinegar.

1 Soak the herring fillets in water overnight. The next day, rinse the herring under running water and then drain. Cut into small pieces and put in a bowl.

2 Put the whole carrots in a pan of cold water, bring to the boil then reduce the heat, cover and simmer for 10–15 minutes, until just tender. Drain and put under cold running water. Set aside.

3 Meanwhile, put the eggs in a pan, cover with cold water and bring to the boil. Reduce the heat and simmer for 10 minutes. When the eggs are cooked, immediately drain and put under cold running water. Set aside.

4 Finely chop the onion and add to the herrings with 15ml/1 tbsp of the mayonnaise. Spread the herring mixture over a flat serving plate measuring about 25cm/10in in diameter.

5 Coarsely grate the carrots, beetroots and apples into small piles or bowls. Add a layer of grated beetroot over the herring mixture and spread 45–60ml/3–4 tbsp mayonnaise on top. Repeat with a layer of grated carrots and mayonnaise and then a layer of grated apple.

6 Finally spread a thin layer of mayonnaise over the top of the salad. Cover with clear film (plastic wrap) and chill in the refrigerator for at least 1 hour or overnight.

7 Just before serving remove the shell from the eggs and grate coarsely. Sprinkle the grated egg all over the salad so that it covers it completely and creates a final layer, then garnish with chopped dill.

Energy 130kcal/544kJ; Protein 12.1g; Carbohydrate 9.3g, of which sugars 8.7g; Fat 5.3g, of which saturates 0.8g; Cholesterol 95mg; Calcium 96mg; Fibre 2.2g; Sodium 1697mg.

Serves 4–8
1 wedge white cabbage, about 250g/9oz
   total weight
250g/9oz can crab meat, preferably Russian
   charka crab meat in its own juice
100g/3¾oz/scant ½ cup mayonnaise
salt
30ml/2 tbsp finely chopped fresh parsley,
   to garnish
bread slices, to serve

Crab Salad
Salat iz Krabov

The famous Russian crab meat, charka, is sold in food shops all over the world. The high quality merits the price. However, inventive Russian housewives found a way to supplement the expensive crab meat by adding finely cut, fresh white cabbage. It is surprisingly good.

1 Finely shred the cabbage, discarding the thick stalk. Put in a large bowl and cover with just boiled water from the kettle.

2 Leave the cabbage to soak for 2–3 minutes. Drain off the water and squeeze the cabbage dry with your hands, transferring the handfuls to a dry bowl as you do so. Set aside and leave to cool.

3 When the cabbage is cool, add the crab meat, in small chunks, and the mayonnaise to the bowl and stir until mixed together. Season with salt to taste and transfer to a serving plate.

4 Garnish the salad with chopped parsley, and serve with bread.

VARIATION
The salad can also be served on pieces of toast, which make a perfect snack to serve with drinks.

Energy 121kcal/501kJ; Protein 6.4g; Carbohydrate 1.9g, of which sugars 1.8g; Fat 9.8g, of which saturates 1.5g; Cholesterol 32mg; Calcium 66mg; Fibre 1g; Sodium 232mg.

Makes 20

25g/1oz fresh yeast

5ml/1 tsp caster (superfine) sugar

50ml/2fl oz/¼ cup warm (37°C/98°F) water

2 egg yolks

250ml/8fl oz/1 cup warm (37°C/98°F) milk

2.5ml/½ tsp salt

175g/6oz/1½ cups plain white (all-purpose) flour

3 egg whites

150ml/¼ pint/⅔ cup rapeseed (canola) oil

For the toppings

slices of smoked salmon

pickled herring, chopped

chopped onion

smetana or crème fraîche

caviar

lemon wedges and dill, to garnish

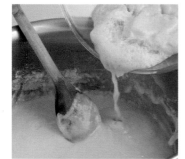

COOK'S TIP
Make the batter for the blinis at least 3 hours before frying, as this allows the yeast to rise fully. Stir the batter 3–4 times while rising.

Russian Pancakes Blini

These little pancakes are delicious served with caviar or smoked salmon, or with smetana, soused herring and chopped onion. Blinis can be served with a topping, or served separately so people can make their own.

1 Put the yeast, sugar and warm water in a small bowl and blend until smooth. Leave in a warm place for 20 minutes until frothy.

2 Mix together the egg yolks, 200ml/6fl oz/¾ cup of the warm milk and the salt in a large bowl. Stir in the yeast mixture and the flour, a little at a time, to form a smooth batter. Leave the batter to rise in a warm place for 4–5 hours, stirring three or four times during that time.

3 Stir the remainder 50ml/2fl oz/¼ cup of the milk into the batter. Whisk the egg whites in a dry bowl until they form soft peaks.

4 Fold the egg whites into the batter and set aside for 30 minutes.

5 Heat the oil in a frying pan and add 25–30ml/1½–2 tbsp of batter for each blini. Fry gently over a medium heat until the batter has set and risen. Turn the blinis over and cook the second side. Continue to cook the remaining batter to make 20 blinis.

6 Your guests can choose their own toppings or you can assemble the blinis yourself. Never use onion with caviar, and if you have real Russian black caviar serve it on its own on the blini, with a spoonful of smetana or crème fraîche on the side.

Energy 89kcal/372kJ; Protein 2g; Carbohydrate 7.6g, of which sugars 0.7g; Fat 5.9g, of which saturates 0.9g; Cholesterol 21mg; Calcium 30mg; Fibre 0.3g; Sodium 16mg.

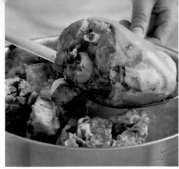

Veal Brawn
Studenj

On the zakuski table, brawn – cooked meat set in jelly – is much appreciated. The pig's trotters are vital, as they provide the jelly in which the veal is set. Brawn should be served with hot mustard or grated horseradish as an accompaniment.

Serves 8–12

1 onion
2 carrots
700g/1lb 10oz veal pieces, on the bone, such as leg
3 pig's trotters (feet), split lengthways
6 white peppercorns
6 black peppercorns
1 bay leaf
about 1 litre/1¾ pints/4 cups water
2 eggs
salt
3–4 fresh parsley sprigs, to garnish
hot mustard or finely grated fresh horseradish, to serve

1 Cut the onion into wedges. Slice one of the carrots. Put the meat, trotters, onion, sliced carrot, 10ml/2 tsp salt, white and black peppercorns and bay leaf in a large pan and add enough water to cover the meat. Bring to the boil and cook for 2–3 minutes. Skim the surface, cover with a lid and cook over a medium heat for 2 hours, until the meat begins to fall off the bones.

2 Using a slotted spoon, remove the meat from the pan. Separate the bones and gristle and return to the pan, putting the meat on a chopping board. Boil the stock with the bone and gristle for a further 1 hour. (This will extract more flavour from the bones and also produce more jelly for the brawn.)

3 Meanwhile, cut the meat into very fine pieces. Put the remaining carrot in a pan of salted water, bring to the boil and cook for 15 minutes, until tender. Drain and leave to cool. When cool enough to handle, thinly slice the carrot.

4 Put the eggs in a pan, cover with cold water and bring to the boil. Reduce the heat to low, cover and simmer for 10 minutes. When the eggs are cooked, immediately drain them and place under cold running water. Remove the shell and slice the egg.

5 Pour the stock through a sieve (strainer) into a measuring jug (cup). Measure the stock then pour into a bowl. Measure the same volume quantity of meat and add to the stock. Season the stock with salt to taste.

VARIATION

As an alternative to veal, you can use either beef or chicken in this dish. Pig's trotters are the traditional way to make the jelly set, and they also give extra flavour to the dish. However, if you can't get hold of them, gelatine can be used, in which case you may need to increase the amount of seasoning.

6 Arrange the slices of carrot and egg in an attractive pattern in the bottom of individual soup plates. Gently pour the meat and stock into the plates, trying to preserve the pattern. Place the plates in the refrigerator for at least 4 hours until the brawn is firm and set.

7 Serve from the bowl or turn out on to a serving plate. Garnish with parsley and accompany with mustard or grated horseradish on the side.

Energy 101kcal/423kJ; Protein 10.6g; Carbohydrate 1.1g, of which sugars 0.9g; Fat 6.1g, of which saturates 2.2g; Cholesterol 51mg; Calcium 9mg; Fibre 0.3g; Sodium 52mg.

Chicken Liver Pâté
Pashtet iz Kurinoj Pecheni

This easy-to-make pâté melts in your mouth and is one of the most popular dishes on the Russian zakuski table. In restaurants the mousse is often served in shells made out of frozen butter on slices of toasted white bread.

Serves 4–6

2 eggs
400g/14oz chicken livers
2.5ml/½ tsp salt
1 onion
45ml/3 tbsp rapeseed (canola) oil
100g/3¾oz/7½ tbsp butter, softened
salt and ground black pepper
bread slices, to serve

For the garnish

2 onions
45ml/3 tbsp rapeseed oil
4–6 sprigs flat leaf parsley

1 Put the eggs in a pan, cover with cold water, and bring to the boil. Reduce the heat to low, and simmer for 10 minutes. When the eggs are cooked, immediately drain and put under cold running water. Remove the shell from the eggs then cut them in half.

2 Rinse the livers under cold running water, put in a small pan and pour over boiling water from the kettle until it just covers the livers. Simmer for 5–8 minutes, until the livers are cooked.

3 Meanwhile, chop the onion. Heat the oil in a small frying pan, add the onion and fry over medium heat, stirring constantly, for 5 minutes until softened and golden brown.

4 Using a slotted spoon, put the livers in a food processor. Add the fried onion, egg halves and butter and process to form a smooth paste. Season the mixture with salt and pepper to taste.

5 Spoon the mixture into a serving bowl, cover and chill in the refrigerator for at least 3–4 hours or overnight.

6 When ready to serve, make the garnish. Finely chop the onions. Heat the oil in a small frying pan, add the onions and fry, stirring occasionally, for about 5 minutes until softened and golden brown. Remove the onions from the pan and leave to cool.

7 Remove the pâté from the refrigerator, garnish with the fried onions and parsley sprigs and serve with slices of bread or toast.

COOK'S TIP
Do not put the pâté mixture in a blender as it is too stiff to mix.

Energy 263kcal/1088kJ; Protein 14.1g; Carbohydrate 0.9g, of which sugars 0.7g; Fat 22.6g, of which saturates 10.3g; Cholesterol 352mg; Calcium 20mg; Fibre 0.1g; Sodium 175mg.

Serves 4
3 potatoes
4 carrots
400g/14oz/3½ cups frozen peas
3 eggs
150g/5oz Salted Cucumbers
175g/6oz/¾ cup mayonnaise
200g/7oz cooked or smoked game, wild
  poultry, turkey or chicken, thinly sliced
2 spring onions (scallions)
salt and ground black pepper
5– 6 fresh dill sprigs, to garnish

COOK'S TIPS

Do not peel the vegetables before cooking as, if you do, they will lose some of their valuable vitamins. Save some slices of carrot, egg and some peas to garnish the salad.

Russian Salad
Salat Olivje

The creamy Russian Salad was devised in the 1880s by Lucien Olivjer, French chef of the Hermitage Restaurant, in Moscow. The dish has since travelled the world under the name of Salade Russe. To serve as they would in Russia, try heaping the salad into a pyramid shape.

1 Put the potatoes in a pan of salted water, bring to the boil then cook for about 20 minutes until tender. Drain and leave to cool. Put the carrots in a separate pan of salted water, bring to the boil and cook for 25 minutes.

2 One minute before the end of the cooking time, add the peas to the pan, return to the boil and continue cooking. Drain and leave to cool.

3 Meanwhile, put the eggs in a pan, cover with cold water, and bring to the boil. Reduce the heat to low, and simmer for 10 minutes. When the eggs are cooked, drain and put under cold running water. Remove the shell then roughly chop the eggs.

4 When the potatoes are cool enough to handle, cut into small dice. Finely dice the carrots. Dice the Salted Cucumbers. Put the potatoes, carrots, chopped eggs, cooked peas and diced cucumbers in a large bowl and mix together.

5 Add the mayonnaise to the vegetables, season with salt and pepper to taste and stir gently together. Turn the salad on to a serving dish.

6 Thinly slice the meat of your choice and place on top of the salad. Thinly slice the spring onions and sprinkle over the top. Serve garnished with dill sprigs.

Energy 455kcal/1890kJ; Protein 28.1g; Carbohydrate 12.8g, of which sugars 5g; Fat 32.8g, of which saturates 5.7g; Cholesterol 387mg; Calcium 162mg; Fibre 4.3g; Sodium 963mg.

Salted Cucumbers Smedomi

Salted cucumbers are the most popular zakuski dish and a cherished ingredient in Russian cooking. This way of serving them, prepared in just a few minutes, arouses all the taste buds. Serve with Russian vodka.

Makes 1kg/2¼lb
1kg/2¼lb mini cucumbers or medium, fresh gherkins, or regular cucumbers
10 blackcurrant leaves
10 garlic cloves
3–4 dill sprigs with flowers
1–2 bay leaves
50g/2oz fresh horseradish, finely diced
20 black peppercorns

For the marinade
1 litre/1¾ pints/4 cups water
2.5ml/½ tsp red or white wine vinegar
45ml/3 tbsp salt

To serve 2 as an appetizer
4–6 salted cucumbers
5ml/1 tsp lemon juice
60ml/4 tbsp smetana or crème fraîche
60ml/4 tbsp clear honey
Russian vodka

1 To prepare the marinade for the cucumbers, put all the ingredients in a pan, bring to the boil then remove from the heat and leave to cool.

2 If you can find mini cucumbers or fresh gherkins, prick all over with a fork, if you are using a large cucumber, cut it into thick fingers.

3 Put the cucumbers into one of several clean, dry glass jars, layering them with blackcurrant leaves, garlic cloves, dill sprigs, bay leaves, horseradish and peppercorns.

4 Pour in the marinade to cover, and seal the jars. Leave to marinate for 5–6 hours. Then store the jars in the refrigerator for at least 2–3 weeks.

5 To serve, place the cucumbers in a serving bowl, cutting into fingers if they were salted whole. Mix the lemon juice with the smetana or crème fraîche. Put the honey in a separate small serving bowl. To eat, dip the cucumbers in honey or smetana or crème fraîche. Serve with vodka.

Energy 503kcal/2086kJ; Protein 8.8g; Carbohydrate 62.7g, of which sugars 61.6g; Fat 25.1g, of which saturates 16.3g; Cholesterol 68mg; Calcium 238mg; Fibre 6.5g; Sodium 80mg.

Makes 1 litre/1¾ pints/4 cups
500g/1¼lb mixed wild mushrooms,
  such as porcini
500ml/17fl oz/generous 2 cups water
25ml/1½ tbsp salt
30ml/2 tbsp red or white wine vinegar
15–30ml/1–2 tbsp sugar
5–6 allspice berries
5–6 black peppercorns
5–6 cloves
2 bay leaves
1 small piece cinnamon stick (optional)
1 garlic clove
2–3 stems fresh dill
2 blackcurrant leaves (optional)

COOK'S TIP
Serve these aromatic sweet-sour
mushrooms on your zakuski table or as
an accompaniment to meat dishes, such
as roast beef.

Marinated Mushrooms
Marinovannye Griby

With the possible exception of Italians, Russians are the
most enthusiastic mushroom pickers in the world.
The best looking mushrooms are preserved in a spicy
marinade and served on the zakuski table during winter.

1 Wipe the mushrooms with kitchen
paper to remove any dirt or traces of
soil. If the mushrooms are large, cut
them in half but leave small
mushrooms whole.

2 Put the mushrooms in a large pan,
add the water and 15ml/1 tbsp salt.
Bring to the boil, then reduce the
heat and simmer for 30 minutes,
stirring occasionally and skimming
the surface.

3 Add the remaining salt, the vinegar,
sugar, allspice, peppercorns, bay
leaves, cinnamon stick and whole
garlic clove to the mushrooms.
Simmer for a further 10 minutes.
Set aside until completely cool.

4 Put the dill and the blackcurrant
leaves, if using, in the bottom of
clean, sterilized glass jars. Pour in
the spiced mushrooms with the
marinade and seal tightly.

5 Store in a cool, dark place or in the
refrigerator. The mushrooms will
keep for 2–3 months and taste better
after at least a few days.

Energy 183kcal/779kJ; Protein 9.2g; Carbohydrate 33.4g, of which sugars 32.4g; Fat 2.5g, of which saturates 0.5g; Cholesterol 0mg; Calcium 48mg; Fibre 5.5g; Sodium 8673mg.

Serves 4–8
1 onion, total weight 150g/5oz
4 medium cooked beetroots (beets)
45ml/3 tbsp rapeseed (canola) oil
30ml/2 tbsp tomato purée (paste)
salt and ground black pepper
12 small pieces rye bread, to serve
finely chopped fresh parsley, to garnish

Beetroot Caviar
Ikra iz Svekly

The delicacies of the sea or Russian inland waters, such as caviar, are often a part of the zakuski table, but chopped, flavoured vegetable dishes, known as 'poor man's caviars', are also popular as less expensive alternatives. As with other vegetable caviars, this beetroot caviar is served on rye bread.

1 Chop the onion and coarsely grate the beetroots. Heat the oil in a medium pan, add the onion and fry gently for 5–8 minutes, until softened and golden brown.

2 Add the grated beetroot to the onion and fry, stirring all the time, for a further 5 minutes.

3 Add the tomato purée to the pan and stir into the onion and beetroot mixture. Cover the pan and simmer gently for 10 minutes.

4 Season the mixture with salt and pepper to taste. Transfer to a bowl and leave to cool.

5 To serve, pile the beetroot caviar on to the rye bread and sprinkle with chopped parsley to garnish.

VARIATION
Add 1–2 crushed garlic cloves to the caviar, either cooked with the onion or, if you prefer it, raw, added with the salt and pepper in step 4.

Energy 60kcal/251kJ; Protein 1.1g; Carbohydrate 4.9g, of which sugars 4.2g; Fat 4.2g, of which saturates 0.5g; Cholesterol 0mg; Calcium 14mg; Fibre 1.1g; Sodium 34mg.

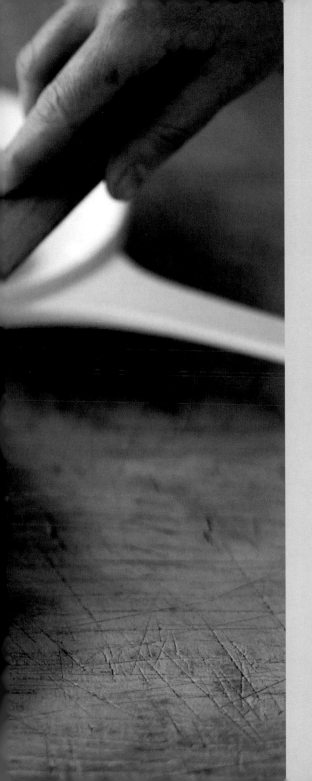

FISH DISHES

Fried Fish with Tartare Sauce

Sole with Vodka Sauce
and Caviar

Fish with Mushroom and
Dill Sauce

Salmon Pie

Fish Kebabs

Roasted Carp with Smetana

Rich and delicious

Fish has always played an important role in Russian cooking. It has been a staple food ever since people first settled along the many rivers and lakes in this huge rural landscape. Religious eating restrictions had its influence on these recipes, as the Orthodox church allowed fish when meat was forbidden during the frequent and strict fasting periods in the religious calendar, and fish was especially prized as a main course at Easter. Today fish is still a very popular ingredient on the Russian lunch or dinner table and in zakuski.

Fish is prepared in so many different and interesting ways in Russia – simmered, roasted, shallow-fried or deep-fried, marinated and served on skewers. These tasty dishes are often accompanied by boiled potatoes that have been tossed with sunflower oil and sprinkled with finely chopped dill, the herb that blends so magically with all kinds of fish. A subtle sauce goes well with many fish dishes – sharp and spicy tartare sauce, earthy and rich mushroom sauce, or white sauce flavoured with a little vodka and cream.

Serves 4

700g/1lb 10oz perch fillet, skinned and boned
5ml/1 tsp salt
15ml/1 tbsp fresh lemon juice
115g/4oz/1 cup plain white
   (all-purpose) flour
150ml/¼ pint/⅔ cup light beer
1 egg white
about 1 litre/1¾ pints/4 cups rapeseed
   (canola) oil
lemon wedges, to garnish
green salad, to serve

For the tartare sauce

3 large pickled gherkins
200g/7fl oz/scant 1 cup mayonnaise
15ml/1 tbsp capers
5ml/1 tsp finely chopped fresh dill
15ml/1 tbsp finely chopped fresh parsley
2.5ml/½ tsp mustard
1.5ml/¼ tsp salt
1.5ml/¼ tsp ground black pepper

Fried Fish with Tartare Sauce Sudak Olrli s Sousom Tartar

Deep-fried fish – usually perch or pike – served with a tartare sauce is a favourite in Russian restaurants. Here a batter is used, but Russians often use smetana.

1 To make the tartare sauce, peel and finely chop the gerkins. Put in a bowl with the mayonnaise, capers, dill, parsley and mustard. Mix together. Add salt and pepper to taste, and transfer to a serving bowl.

2 Cut the fish fillets into pieces measuring about 3cm/1¼in and put on a plate. Sprinkle the fish pieces with the salt and lemon juice.

3 Put the flour and beer in a bowl and whisk together until it forms a smooth batter. In a separate bowl, whisk the egg white until it stands in soft peaks then fold into the batter.

4 Heat the oil in a deep fryer to 180°C/350°F or until a cube of bread browns in 1 minute. Dip and turn the fish pieces in the batter and then drop into the hot oil. Fry for 1–2 minutes, until golden. Using a slotted spoon, remove from the pan and drain on kitchen paper.

5 Serve the fish hot with lemon wedges and the tartare sauce.

Energy 719kcal/2986kJ; Protein 36.7g; Carbohydrate 24.3g, of which sugars 2.1g; Fat 53.4g, of which saturates 7.6g; Cholesterol 118mg; Calcium 95mg; Fibre 1.8g; Sodium 352mg.

Serves 4

500–600g/1lb 4oz–1lb 6oz sole, flounder or
  plaice fillets
200ml/7fl oz/scant 1 cup fish stock
60ml/4 tbsp caviar
salt
4 lemon wedges and fresh dill, to garnish
hot boiled potatoes, to serve

For the vodka sauce
25–40g/1–1½oz/2–3 tbsp butter
5–6 shallots, finely diced
5ml/1 tsp plain white (all-purpose) flour
200ml/7fl oz/scant 1 cup double
  (heavy) cream
200ml/7fl oz/scant 1 cup fish stock
100ml/3½fl oz/scant ½ cup dry white wine
30ml/2 tbsp vodka
salt and ground black pepper

Sole with Vodka Sauce and Caviar
Morskoj Jazyk s

Caviar was once served only with silver spoons to protect the taste. Today, caviar is served on white buttered toast or Blinis, or as a luxurious garnish to a delicious fish.

1 Season the fish fillets with salt. Roll up and secure each fillet with a cocktail stick (toothpick).

2 Heat the stock in a small pan. Place the fish rolls in the pan, cover and simmer for 5–8 minutes, until the fish is tender. Remove from the pan and keep warm.

3 Meanwhile, make the sauce. Melt the butter in a pan, add the shallots and fry gently for 3–5 minutes, until softened but not browned. Add the flour and stir until well mixed.

4 Gradually add the cream and stock until smooth. Slowly bring to the boil, stirring, until the sauce bubbles. Reduce the heat and simmer for 3–5 minutes, until the sauce thickens. Remove the shallots with a slotted spoon. Add the wine and vodka and bring to the boil. Season with salt and pepper to taste.

5 Pour the sauce over the base of four warmed plates. Place the fish rolls on top and add a spoonful of caviar to each. Garnish with lemon and dill and serve with hot boiled potatoes.

Energy 470kcal/1952kJ; Protein 27.9g; Carbohydrate 3.2g, of which sugars 1.9g; Fat 35g, of which saturates 20.4g; Cholesterol 188mg; Calcium 103mg; Fibre 0.3g; Sodium 548mg.

Fish with Mushroom and Dill Sauce
Sudak s Gribnym Sousom

Dill and flat leaf parsley are the herbs most commonly used in Russian cuisine, and both go superbly with most fish dishes. In this recipe the fish is accompanied by a creamy mushroom sauce with a rich taste of fresh dill.

Serves 4

4 perch fillets, total weight 500–600g/1lb
  4oz–1lb 6oz, skinned
5ml/1 tsp salt
plain white (all-purpose) flour, to coat
35–50g/1½–2oz/3–4 tbsp butter
hot boiled new potatoes, to serve

For the dill sauce

2 onions
20 fresh mushrooms
45ml/3 tbsp rapeseed (canola) oil
15ml/1 tbsp plain white
  (all-purpose) flour
200ml/7fl oz/scant 1 cup fish stock
250ml/8fl oz/1 cup double (heavy) cream
100ml/3½fl oz/scant ½ cup smetana or
  crème fraîche
100ml/3½fl oz/scant ½ cup dry white wine
1 large bunch fresh dill
1–2 dashes mushroom or soy sauce
salt and white pepper

VARIATION

Any other firm-fleshed white fish, such as cod or haddock, can be used instead of the perch, and you can substitute frozen or wild mushrooms, such as porcini, for the sauce.

1 To make the sauce, chop the onions and slice the mushrooms. In a large frying pan, heat the oil, add the onions and fry, over a medium high heat, for 3–5 minutes until softened but not browned. Add the sliced mushrooms and fry for a further 5–10 minutes.

2 Meanwhile, season the fish fillets with the salt and coat with the flour. Heat the butter in a large non-stick frying pan over a medium heat. Add the fish and fry for 3 minutes on each side or until golden brown and crisp.

3 Sprinkle the flour into the onions and mushrooms and stir until mixed. Gradually stir in the stock until smooth. Slowly bring to the boil, stirring all the time, until the sauce boils and thickens.

4 Stir the cream and smetana or crème fraîche into the sauce. Reduce the heat and simmer for 3 minutes.

5 Meanwhile, chop the dill. Add the white wine to the sauce and season with the soy sauce, salt and pepper to taste. Stir in the chopped dill.

6 Spoon the sauce over the fish in the pan, reheat gently and serve with hot boiled new potatoes.

Energy 706kcal/2924kJ; Protein 31.2g; Carbohydrate 15.6g, of which sugars 7.5g; Fat 56.3g, of which saturates 30.7g; Cholesterol 191mg; Calcium 98mg; Fibre 1.8g; Sodium 137mg.

Salmon Pie
Kulebjaka s Semgoj

This Russian speciality is a puff-pastry pie filled with cured salmon, hard-boiled eggs and rice. Pastry of all kinds is very popular in Eastern Europe and it is especially enjoyed in Russia. In the times of the Tsar, elaborate pastries were sent as party invitations and the skills of a hostess were always measured by the quality of her pastry. These days, good quality, butter-rich, ready-made pastry is an acceptable substitute for homemade.

Serves 4

4 eggs
50g/2oz/¼ cup long grain rice
300g/11oz gravlax or smoked salmon
15g/½oz/¼ cup chopped fresh dill
45ml/3 tbsp smetana or crème fraîche
1 sheet ready-made chilled puff pastry,
   measuring about 40x20cm/16x8in
salt and ground black pepper
1 egg yolk
5ml/1 tsp water
15ml/1 tbsp fresh white breadcrumbs

1 Put the eggs in a pan, cover with cold water, and bring to the boil. Reduce the heat to low, and simmer for 10 minutes. When the eggs are cooked, immediately drain and put under cold running water. Remove the shell then chop the eggs into small pieces.

2 Meanwhile, bring a large pan of salted water to the boil, add the rice and stir to loosen the grains at the bottom of the pan. Simmer for about 20 minutes, until tender. Drain into a sieve (strainer) and rinse under cold water.

3 Cut the gravlax or smoked salmon into strips and put in a large bowl. Add the eggs, rice, dill and smetana or crème fraîche and mix together. Season with salt and pepper to taste.

4 Preheat the oven to 220°C/425°F/Gas 7. Put the sheet of pastry on a dampened baking tray. Spread the filling lengthways on one half of the pastry sheet. Brush the edges with water and fold the other side over to enclose the filling. Seal together by pressing with a fork along the join. It should be like a tightly packed loaf.

5 Whisk together the egg yolk and water. Brush the pastry with the glaze and make some small holes in the top with a fork. Sprinkle the breadcrumbs over the top. Bake the pie in the oven for 12–15 minutes, until golden brown. Leave the baked pie to rest for 5–10 minutes then cut into slices and serve.

COOK'S TIP
Instead of mixing the filling ingredients together, add them in layers. Start with the rice, then the salmon, smetana or crème fraîche, eggs and dill. Season between the layers.

Energy 624kcal/2606kJ; Protein 32.7g; Carbohydrate 45.6g, of which sugars 1.6g; Fat 36.4g, of which saturates 5.6g; Cholesterol 280mg; Calcium 121mg; Fibre 0.3g; Sodium 1786mg.

Serves 4

30ml/2 tbsp fresh lemon juice
60ml/4 tbsp smetana or crème fraîche
1kg/2¼lb firm white fish fillets, such as a
  halibut or monkfish
25g/1oz/2 tbsp butter
salt

For the garnish

25g/1oz/2 tbsp butter
4 spring onions (scallions)
1 lemon
4 tomatoes
30ml/2 tbsp finely chopped fresh parsley

VARIATION

In Russia, sturgeon is often used for this
dish but any firm, white fish is suitable.
You can also use salmon.

Fish Kebabs
Sjaslik iz Ryby

To cook fish outside on skewers over coals or a wood fire
and then serve with squeezed lemon and fresh tomato,
is an ancient Russian tradition. Although incredibly
simple to prepare, this dish is a popular choice in many
Caucasian restaurants in Russia.

1 Heat a barbecue or preheat the
oven to 240ºC/475ºF/Gas 9.

2 To make the marinade, put the
lemon juice and smetana or crème
fraîche in a large bowl and mix
together. Cut the fish into small
chunks, season with salt, add to the
marinade and stir to coat all over.
Leave for 10–15 minutes for the fish
to absorb the flavours.

3 Melt the butter in a small pan.
Thread the fish chunks tightly
together on to four metal skewers or
wooden skewers that have been
soaked in water. Pre-heat the grill
(broiler) if using.

4 Cook the skewers on the barbecue,
in the oven or under the grill for
about 10 minutes, or until the fish is
golden brown and firm. Baste the fish
occasionally during cooking with the
melted butter and the remaining
marinade. Turn the skewers
occasionally so that the fish cooks
on all sides.

5 Meanwhile, prepare the garnish.
Finely slice the spring onions and cut
the lemon and tomatoes into wedges.
To serve, put the skewers on a large
serving dish and sprinkle over the
spring onions and chopped parsley.
Arrange the lemon and tomatoes
wedges around the fish skewers.

Energy 303kcal/1267kJ; Protein 46.1g; Carbohydrate 0.4g, of which sugars 0.4g; Fat 12.9g, of which saturates 7.6g; Cholesterol 145mg; Calcium 32mg; Fibre 0g; Sodium 191mg.

Serves 4–6

40g/1½oz/3 tbsp butter, plus extra
  for greasing
1 whole carp, bream or trout, gutted,
  total weight 1–1.5kg/2¼–3¼lb
45ml/3 tbsp plain white
  (all-purpose) flour
300ml/½ pint/1¼ cups smetana or
  crème fraîche
100ml/3½fl oz/scant ½ cup water
salt and ground black pepper
5–6 fresh parsley sprigs, to garnish
torn lettuce leaves and hot boiled
  potatoes, to serve

VARIATION
In Russia, mayonnaise is sometimes used
instead of the smetana.

Roasted Carp with Smetana Ryba Zapechennaja v Smetane

Roasting a whole fish in the oven, covered with smetana, is an old Russian method. A more modern way is to use fish fillets, instead of a whole fish, and bake them in ramekin dishes on top of a base of boiled buckwheat. Both are equally delicious.

1 Preheat the oven to 230°C/450°F/Gas 8. Generously grease an ovenproof dish with butter. Season the whole fish on the inside and outside with salt and pepper then coat both sides in the flour. Place the fish in the prepared dish.

2 Melt the butter in a small pan. Spread the smetana or crème fraîche over the fish, making sure that it covers it completely.

3 Pour the melted butter over the fish and pour the water around it.

4 Bake in the preheated oven. A 40–50cm/16–20in thick fish will need around 20 minutes and a 60cm/24in thick fish will need 30 minutes.

5 The fish is cooked when the flesh is white and not translucent. Test by inserting a fork in the backbone of the fish where it is thickest.

6 Serve the fish in portions straight from the dish, garnished with parsley and accompanied with torn salad leaves and boiled potatoes tossed in a little oil and salt.

Energy 395kcal/1640kJ; Protein 22.3g; Carbohydrate 7.1g, of which sugars 1.2g; Fat 31.1g, of which saturates 18.1g; Cholesterol 149mg; Calcium 96mg; Fibre 0.2g; Sodium 102mg.

MEAT, POULTRY AND GAME

Beef Stroganoff

Kebabs with Plum Sauce

Little Beef Dumplings

Burgers with Buckwheat
and Fried Onions

Little Beef Pies

Rabbit in Smetana

Venison Ragoût

Baked Lamb

Uzbekistani Pilaff

Chicken Burgers with
Mushroom Sauce

Chicken Kiev

Chicken with Walnut Sauce

Roast Goose with Apples

Sustaining meats

The large wood-burning stove that takes up a big part of most Russian cottages in the countryside, and was kept alight the whole year round, is perfect for roasting meat. Russians are meat-lovers and they like their meat and poultry roasted whole, just as it was in the old days. The recipes of this vast country make full use of the beef and lamb from the farmer's fields, game from the forests and chickens from the smallholder's backyard. Many dishes call for long cooking in a casserole in the oven. Most of these dishes also contain mixtures of vegetables and grains to add bulk and make a complete meal in one pot. Mushrooms, tomatoes, potatoes and cabbage are often included for colour and flavour as well as their nutritional qualities, and most of these ingredients would have been available to country people for centuries. The addition of sour cream or smetana, as in the rabbit dish Krolik v Smetane, gives these meat dishes a particularly Russian taste.

Serves 4
40–50g/1½–2oz/3–4 tbsp butter
500g/1¼lb beef fillet, very thinly sliced
salt and ground black pepper
Salted Cucumbers, diced, to serve

For the sauce
2–3 onions, thinly sliced
30–45ml/2–3 tbsp rapeseed (canola) oil
1 chicken stock (bouillon) cube
45ml/3 tbsp tomato purée (paste)
15ml/1 tbsp plain white (all-purpose) flour
2–3 bay leaves
4–5 black peppercorns
300ml/½ pint/1¼ cups water
200ml/7fl oz/scant 1 cup double
   (heavy) cream
100ml/3½fl oz/scant ½ cup smetana or
   crème fraîche

For the fried potatoes
6–8 potatoes, peeled and very thinly sliced
90–105ml/6–7 tbsp rapeseed (canola) oil
salt

Beef Stroganoff
Bef Stroganov

This famous dish was created at the time of Catherine the Great by Count Alexander Sergeyevich Stroganov. The Count invited poor students into his house, and served this casserole with fried potatoes and Salted Cucumbers.

1 First make the sauce. Heat the oil in a medium pan. Add the sliced onions and fry over a medium heat for 3–5 minutes. Crumble the stock cube into the onions and fry for a further 1–2 minutes.

2 Add the tomato purée to the pan, then the flour and stir well together. Add the bay leaves and peppercorns and then gradually stir in the water and the cream until smooth. Slowly bring to the boil, stirring all the time, until the sauce boils and thickens. Cover and simmer for 10 minutes. Stir in the smetana or crème fraîche.

3 Meanwhile, fry the potatoes. Heat the oil in a large frying pan. Add the sliced potatoes and fry for

10–15 minutes, turning occasionally. Cover the pan and cook for a further 10–15 minutes, until tender. Season the potatoes with salt to taste.

4 To cook the beef, heat the butter in a frying pan. Add the slices of beef, in batches, and cook quickly, over a high heat, for about 1 minute until browned. Transfer to a plate, season with salt and pepper and keep warm. Repeat with the remaining beef until all the meat is cooked.

5 When you are ready to serve, reheat the sauce, add the beef to the sauce and heat through gently for 2–3 minutes. Serve immediately with the fried potatoes and accompanied with diced Salted Cucumbers.

Energy 919kcal/3810kJ; Protein 32.5g; Carbohydrate 36g, of which sugars 11.7g; Fat 72.6g, of which saturates 34.6g; Cholesterol 194mg; Calcium 94mg; Fibre 3.4g; Sodium 177mg.

Kebabs with Plum Sauce
Sjaslik s Sousom Tkemal

Serves 4

800g–1kg/1¾–2¼lb beef fillet
1 onion, finely sliced
200ml/7fl oz/scant 1 cup red wine
15g/½oz/1 tbsp butter
salt and ground black pepper
lemon wedges, to garnish
green salad and cooked rice, to serve

For the Plum Sauce

300g/11oz fresh green or red plums
400ml/14fl oz/1⅔ cups water
2 garlic cloves
45ml/3 tbsp chopped fresh
   coriander (cilantro)
small pinch of cayenne pepper
salt

VARIATION
You can cook skewers of lamb, such as
lamb fillet or boneless loin of lamb, in the
same way.

At weekends, Russians love to go on a picnic. Family
members, friends and colleagues are all invited to go to
sjasliki – cooking food on skewers. The best sjaslik are
made over the glowing cinders left from an open fire.

1 Cut the meat into 3–4cm/1¼–1½in square chunks. Put in a large bowl and season with salt and pepper. Add the onion and wine to the beef and mix. Cover the bowl with clear film (plastic wrap) and leave in the refrigerator for at least 3 hours.

2 For the sauce, put the plums in a small pan. Add the water, bring to the boil, reduce the heat then cover and simmer for 20 minutes. Remove the plums from the pan and set aside. Reserve the liquid.

3 When the plums are cool, remove the stones (pits) and put the flesh in a food processor. Add the garlic, coriander and about 75ml/5 tbsp of

the plum liquid and blend to a smooth purée. Add more liquid to the purée, a little at a time, until it is the consistency of thick cream. Season with cayenne pepper and salt to taste.

4 Heat a barbecue or preheat the grill (broiler). Melt the butter. Thread the marinated meat chunks on to long metal skewers.

5 Brush the meat with the melted butter. Cook the skewers for about 10–15 minutes, turning to cook the meat on all sides.

6 Serve the skewers with the plum sauce and a green salad, on a bed of boiled rice. Garnish with lemon.

Energy 325kcal/1364kJ; Protein 43.4g; Carbohydrate 8.2g, of which sugars 7.8g; Fat 12.5g, of which saturates 5.6g; Cholesterol 122mg; Calcium 48mg; Fibre 2g; Sodium 95mg.

Little Beef Dumplings
Peljmeni

These tiny Siberian dumplings are traditionally accompanied by red wine vinegar, melted butter and ground black pepper. Russians expect to eat about 40 pelmeni at a time, but this is, of course, not obligatory. It is customary to make pelmeni in advance and freeze them, to be cooked from frozen as needed. Leftover pelmeni are delicious fried in butter.

Makes 80–100
Serves 4–6
2 eggs
150ml/¼ pint/⅔ cup water
15ml/1 tbsp rapeseed (canola) oil
2.5ml/½ tsp salt
360g/12½oz/3⅛ cups plain white (all-purpose) flour, plus extra for dusting

For the filling
1 onion, total weight 100g/3¾oz
200g/7oz minced (ground) beef
200g/7oz minced (ground) pork
7.5ml/1½ tsp salt
2–2.5ml/⅓–½ tsp ground black pepper
red wine vinegar, melted butter, salt and ground black pepper, and smetana (optional), to serve

COOK'S TIP
The best pelmeni are always handmade but, if you want to save time, you can roll the dough through a pasta machine and cut the pieces into rounds using a 5cm/2in round cutter. Fill them with the meat mixture and seal by pressing the edges firmly together.

1 First make the pastry. Put the eggs, water, oil, salt and half of the flour in a food processor and process until well blended. Add the remaining flour, in batches, to form a smooth pastry. Turn the pastry on to a lightly floured surface and knead for 5 minutes. Put in a plastic bag and leave to rest for 30 minutes, or overnight, in a cold place.

2 To make the filling, finely grate the onion and put in a bowl. Add the minced beef and pork, salt and pepper and mix together. Set aside.

3 To make the dumplings, cut the pastry into eight pieces. Work with one piece at a time, keeping the remaining pieces in the plastic bag to prevent them from drying out. On a floured surface, roll the piece of pastry into a roll, the thickness of a finger. Cut the roll into 10–12 small pieces.

4 Flatten out each piece to a round, about 3cm/1¼in in diameter, and then roll out into a thinner round, 5–6cm/2–2½in in diameter. Spread each round with 5m/1 tsp of the meat mixture, leaving a small uncovered edge. Fold and pinch together the rounds to form a half-moon shape.

5 As you make the dumplings, put them on a floured baking sheet. When the sheet is full, put it in the freezer. When frozen, transfer the dumplings to a plastic bag and keep frozen until required.

6 When you are ready to serve the dumplings, take the amount you need from the freezer and put in a pan of lightly salted boiling water. Simmer until the dumplings float to the surface then simmer for a further 1 minute. Using a slotted spoon, scoop out of the water and serve immediately, sprinkled with vinegar, melted butter, salt and pepper. A small amount of the cooking water and smetana may also be added to taste, if wished.

Energy 381kcal/1605kJ; Protein 20.9g; Carbohydrate 47.9g, of which sugars 1.8g; Fat 13.1g, of which saturates 4.4g; Cholesterol 105mg; Calcium 103mg; Fibre 2.1g; Sodium 74mg.

Burgers with Buckwheat and Fried Onions
Kotletki s Grechkoj i Lukom

Kotletki are Russia's fast food. Russians love them and eat them for both lunch and dinner. Although they can be bought ready-made from the meat counter in the supermarkets, the best kotletki are home-made. Here they are served with buckwheat and fried onions. Buckwheat has a nutty taste and a slightly chewy texture.

Serves 4

1 potato
1 onion
300g/11oz minced (ground) beef
300g/11oz minced (ground) pork
5ml/1 tsp salt
heaped 1.5ml/¼ tsp ground black pepper
75g/3oz/1½ cups fresh breadcrumbs
25–40g/1–1½oz/2–3 tbsp butter
30ml/2 tbsp rapeseed (canola) oil
100ml/3½fl oz/scant ½ cup smetana or
   crème fraîche and 4–8 small gherkins,
   to serve

For the buckwheat

350g/12oz/1¾ cups whole buckwheat
   grains
1 litre/1¾ pints/4 cups boiling water
5ml/1 tsp salt
2 large onions
45–60ml/3–4 tbsp sunflower oil

VARIATION

The grated potato in the burgers can be replaced with two slices of stale white bread. Remove the crusts and soak in 100ml/3½fl oz/scant ½ cup milk for 5 minutes, until soft.

1 To make the burgers, grate the potato and onion and put in a large bowl. Add the beef, pork, salt and pepper and mix well together until the mixture is smooth. Rinse a chopping board in cold water. Form the meat mixture into 10–12, equal-sized, 2cm/¾in thick burgers and place them on the chopping board. (Using a wet surface prevents the burgers from sticking.)

2 Spread the breadcrumbs on to a plate. Turn the burgers in the breadcrumbs until coated and then place them on a plate or dry chopping board. Set aside.

3 To cook the buckwheat. Heat a small frying pan until hot, add the buckwheat and dry-fry for 1–2 minutes. Transfer to a medium pan and add the boiling water and salt. Stir, cover with a lid and cook over a medium heat for 20–30 minutes, until the grains are soft and have absorbed all the water.

4 Meanwhile, cook the burgers. Heat the butter and oil in a medium frying pan until hot and the butter has melted. Add three or four burgers at a time and fry, over a medium heat, for 2–3 minutes on each side. Remove from the pan and continue to cook the remaining burgers in the same way. When all the burgers are cooked, return them to the pan, cover with a lid and cook, over a low heat, for 10 minutes.

5 Meanwhile, prepare the onions for the buckwheat. Slice the onions into rings. Heat the oil in a medium frying pan, add the onions and fry, stirring frequently, over a low heat for 5 minutes, or until softened and golden brown.

6 When the buckwheat is cooked, drain and return to the pan. Add the fried onions and stir together. Arrange the burgers in a row on a serving dish and put the buckwheat along each side. Serve hot, with smetana or crème fraîche and gherkins.

Energy 839kcal/3515kJ; Protein 38.9g; Carbohydrate 85.9g, of which sugars 9g; Fat 40.2g, of which saturates 12.9g; Cholesterol 108mg; Calcium 88mg; Fibre 2.9g; Sodium 1284mg.

Little Beef Pies
Pirojki Nachinkoj iz Mjasa

These golden little pastries are often served on the zakuski table and also as an accompaniment to soups. In this recipe they are filled with beef, but other fillings can be used such as salmon, potato or cabbage.

Makes 24 little pies
Serves 6–8
1 large onion
30–45ml/2–3 tbsp rapeseed (canola) oil
400g/14oz minced (ground) beef
100ml/3½fl oz/scant ½ cup beef stock
30ml/2 tbsp smetana or crème fraîche
1 egg
salt and ground black pepper

For the dough
50g/2oz/¼ cup butter
200ml/7fl oz/scant 1 cup milk
45ml/3 tbsp water
1 small (US medium) egg plus 1 egg yolk
2.5ml/½ tsp salt
7.5ml/1½ tsp caster (superfine) sugar
5g/⅛oz easy-blend (rapid-rise) dried yeast
400g/14oz/3½ cups plain
  (all-purpose) flour

1 To make the filling, finely chop the onion. Heat the oil in a medium frying pan, add the onion and fry for 5 minutes until softened and golden brown. Add the beef and fry, stirring frequently, for about 10 minutes, until browned, then add the stock and smetana or crème fraîche to the pan. Stir together then cover and simmer gently, stirring occasionally, for 10–15 minutes. Leave to cool.

2 Meanwhile, put the egg in a pan, cover with cold water and bring to the boil. Reduce the heat to low, and simmer for 10 minutes. When the egg is cooked, immediately drain and put under cold running water. Remove the shell from the egg then finely chop. When the beef has cooled, stir in the chopped egg. Season with salt and pepper to taste. Set aside, while you make the dough.

3 To make the dough, melt the butter in a pan. Add the milk and water and heat it to 45°C/110°F. Remove from the heat. Whisk the whole egg in a bowl with the salt and sugar. Add the warm milk mixture.

4 Mix the yeast with the flour and stir, a little at a time, into the warm egg mixture. Knead the dough in the bowl for 5 minutes. Cover with a dish towel and leave to rise in a warm place for 30 minutes, until doubled in size.

5 Grease a large baking sheet. Turn the dough on to a lightly floured surface and knead for 2–3 minutes. Cut the dough into 24 equal-sized pieces and form each piece into a ball. Leave to rest for 5–10 minutes. Flatten each ball to a round measuring 10cm/4in in diameter. Spread 25ml/1½ tbsp of the beef filling in the centre of each round of dough. Fold together and seal the edges at the top. Put them, upside-down with the join facing down, on the baking sheet.

6 Preheat the oven to 230°C/450°F/Gas 8. Whisk the egg yolk with 15ml/1 tbsp water and brush on top of the pies. Leave to rest for 20 minutes. Bake the pies in the oven for 12–13 minutes, until golden. Transfer to a wire rack and leave to cool.

Energy 411kcal/1719kJ; Protein 17.4g; Carbohydrate 41.7g, of which sugars 3.4g; Fat 20.5g, of which saturates 9g; Cholesterol 117mg; Calcium 120mg; Fibre 1.7g; Sodium 108mg.

Serves 4–6
1 rabbit, total weight about 1.5kg/3¼lb,
　cleaned and skinned
40g/1½oz/3 tbsp butter
12 shallots
45–60ml/3–4 tbsp water
200ml/7fl oz/scant 1 cup beef stock
300ml/½ pint/1¼ cups smetana or
　crème fraîche
15g/½oz/¼ cup finely chopped fresh
　parsley, plus 4–5 sprigs, to garnish
salt and ground black pepper
boiled potatoes, rice or pasta, to serve

COOK'S TIP
If you have difficulty in buying rabbit from
a supermarket, you can order it from a
butcher or often find it at a food market.
Chicken can be used instead.

Rabbit in Smetana
Krolik v Smetane

Smetana, a sour cream, is an ingredient in many
Russian dishes. Rabbit cooked in a sauce of smetana
acquires a delicate, mild flavour. Boiled potatoes are the
traditional accompaniment.

1 Cut the rabbit meat into bitesize
chunks. Heat the butter in a large
frying pan until melted and beginning
to turn brown. Add the rabbit pieces
and fry over a medium heat, stirring
occasionally, for 10 minutes, until
browned on all sides. Season the
rabbit with salt and pepper.

2 Add the shallots and water and half
the beef stock to the pan, cover and
cook over a low heat for 1–1½ hours,
until the meat is tender. If necessary,
add a little additional water.

3 Put the rest of the beef stock, the
smetana or crème fraîche and the
chopped parsley in a jug (pitcher)
and mix together. Add the mixture to
the meat, bring to the boil then
reduce the heat and simmer for
10–15 minutes.

4 To serve, put the meat on to a
warmed serving dish and spoon over
the sauce. Garnish the rabbit with
parsley sprigs and accompany with
boiled potatoes, rice or pasta.

Energy 436kcal/1809kJ; Protein 33.9g; Carbohydrate 6.7g, of which sugars 5g; Fat 30.5g, of which saturates 19.5g; Cholesterol 193mg; Calcium 121mg; Fibre 1.4g; Sodium 129mg.

Venison Ragoût
Ragu iz Oleniny

Bear meat was originally used in this recipe, which dates from the times when bear was hunted in Russia, but venison can be substituted. In some Russian restaurants today bear ragoût made with imported meat is served.

Serves 4

600g/1lb 6oz venison or elk fillet
2 onions
500g/1¼lb turnips
5–6 juniper berries
40g/1½oz/3 tbsp butter
30ml/2 tbsp rapeseed (canola) oil
1 beef stock (bouillon) cube
60–75ml/4–5 tbsp tomato purée (paste)
15ml/1 tbsp plain white (all-purpose) flour
2–3 bay leaves
4–5 black peppercorns
500ml/17fl oz/generous 2 cups water
300ml/½ pint/1¼ cups double
  (heavy) cream
salt and ground black pepper
mashed or boiled potatoes and Marinated
  Mushrooms, to serve

VARIATION
If you use bear fillet, increase the cooking time by about 1½ hours.

1 Cut the meat into chunky pieces. Chop the onions, dice the turnips and crush the juniper berries. Heat the butter and oil in a flameproof casserole. Add the meat and fry, stirring frequently, for about 10 minutes, until browned on all sides.

2 Add the onions to the pan and fry for 3–5 minutes. Add the turnips and fry, stirring all the time, for a further 5 minutes. Crumble in the stock cube and add the tomato purée.

3 Sprinkle the flour over the meat and fry, stirring all the time, for 1 minute. Add the crushed juniper berries, bay leaves, peppercorns and gradually stir in the water. Bring to the boil then reduce the heat, cover and simmer for about 1½ hours, until the meat is tender.

4 Stir the cream into the pan and cook for a further 10 minutes. Season the ragoût with salt and pepper to taste and serve hot with boiled or mashed potatoes and Marinated Mushrooms.

Energy 758kcal/3148kJ; Protein 37.6g; Carbohydrate 19.1g, of which sugars 13.7g; Fat 60.7g, of which saturates 32.4g; Cholesterol 199mg; Calcium 139mg; Fibre 4.7g; Sodium 200mg.

Serves 4
600g/1lb 6oz potatoes
1 large onion
1 aubergine (eggplant)
1 mild chilli
3 garlic cloves
800g/1¾lb boneless lamb
45ml/3 tbsp chopped fresh parsley
4 bay leaves
6–8 black peppercorns
45ml/3 tbsp chopped fresh
   coriander (cilantro)
50g/2oz/¼ cup butter
75ml/5 tbsp tomato purée (paste)
1 litre/1¾ pints/4 cups beef stock
3 tomatoes
salt and ground black pepper

VARIATION
The aubergines can be replaced with
2 large onions.

Baked Lamb
Chanachi po-Gruzinski

In Russian restaurants, this delicious all-in-one dish of lamb with potatoes, aubergines and tomatoes, is cooked in individual dishes, which are brought straight from the oven to the table. It is very simple to make.

1 Preheat the oven to 180°C/350°F/ Gas 4. First prepare the vegetables. Roughly dice the potatoes, chop the onion, and slice the aubergine. Chop the chilli, discarding the core and seeds. Chop the garlic. Put the potatoes and onions in a greased roasting pan.

2 Cut the lamb into bitesize chunks. Sprinkle the lamb, aubergine, chilli, parsley, bay leaves, peppercorns, coriander and garlic evenly over the potatoes.

3 Melt the butter in a small pan. Add the tomato purée and fry for 1 minute. Stir in the stock, a little at a time, and bring to the boil. Season with salt and pepper to taste.

4 Pour the tomato sauce over the meat and the vegetables. Bake in the oven for about 1 hour, until the meat and vegetables are tender. Meanwhile, slice the tomatoes. Add the tomatoes to the pan, return to the oven and bake for a further 10 minutes. Serve hot.

Energy 631kcal/2640kJ; Protein 45.3g; Carbohydrate 38.6g, of which sugars 13.9g; Fat 34g, of which saturates 17.2g; Cholesterol 179mg; Calcium 94mg; Fibre 5.8g; Sodium 324mg.

Serves 4

600g/1lb 6oz lean boneless lamb steak
60–75ml/4–5 tbsp rapeseed (canola) oil
700ml/1 pint 3½fl oz/scant 3 cups water
5ml/1 tsp salt
2 carrots
2 onions
350–400g/12–14oz/1¾–2 cups long
  grain rice
1 whole garlic, with the dry outer skin
  removed, but left intact
5 sprigs fresh parsley, to garnish

COOK'S TIP
The Uzbekistanis rinse their rice several
times in water before cooking it. This
reduces the amount of starch and
prevents the rice from becoming sticky.

Uzbekistani Pilaff
Uzbekskij Plov

In Uzbekistan a pilaff is the classic dish for entertaining,
and can be varied in endless ways. Traditionally everyone
eats directly from the same large serving dish.

1 Cut the lamb into bitesize pieces.
Heat 15ml/1 tbsp of the oil in a
flameproof casserole. Add the lamb
and fry, stirring frequently. for about
10 minutes, until brown on all sides.

2 Add the water and salt to the pan,
bring to the boil then reduce the heat
and simmer for about 40 minutes,
until the meat is just tender.

3 Meanwhile, finely dice the carrots
and finely chop the onion. Heat the
remaining oil in a separate pan. Add

the carrots and onions and stir-fry
for about 5 minutes, until softened.
Add the rice and stir-fry for about
1 minute, until translucent.

4 Transfer the rice mixture to the
lamb and add the whole garlic.
Bring to the boil then reduce the
heat, cover and simmer for about
20 minutes, until the rice is tender
and has absorbed most of the liquid.

5 Serve the pilaff heaped on to a
warmed dish, garnished with parsley.

Energy 735kcal/3065kJ; Protein 37.2g; Carbohydrate 81.7g, of which sugars 9.8g; Fat 28.6g, of which saturates 9.2g; Cholesterol 114mg; Calcium 66mg; Fibre 2.9g; Sodium 150mg.

Chicken Burgers with Mushroom Sauce
Kotlety Pojarskie s Gribnym Sousom

Burgers made with minced meat, fish or vegetables, are everyday food in Russia and the Russians love them. Chicken burgers are served in restaurants coated with crisp snippets of toasted bread rather than breadcrumbs, and are delicious eaten with puréed potatoes.

Serves 4

600g/1lb 6oz minced (ground)
   chicken breast
1 egg
75g/3oz/1½ cups fresh white
   breadcrumbs
40g/1½oz/3 tbsp butter
salt and ground black pepper

For the mushroom sauce

25g/1oz dried sliced mushrooms, such as
   porcini, soaked for 2–3 hours
700ml/1 pint 3½fl oz/scant 3 cups water
1 onion, chopped
30ml/2 tbsp rapeseed (canola) oil
15ml/1 tbsp plain white
   (all-purpose) flour
45ml/3 tbsp smetana or crème fraîche
salt and ground black pepper

For the puréed potatoes

1kg/2¼lb floury potatoes
200–250ml/7–8fl oz/scant 1–1 cup
   warm milk
15g/½oz/1 tbsp butter
salt

1 For the mushroom sauce, put the soaked mushrooms and the water in a pan and simmer for 40 minutes. Using a slotted spoon, remove the mushrooms from the pan, reserving the water.

2 Heat the oil in a large frying pan, add the onion and fry, stirring frequently, for 3 minutes, or until golden brown. Add the mushrooms and fry, stirring all the time, for a further 5 minutes. Sprinkle the flour over the mushrooms and stir until mixed.

3 Gradually stir all the reserved water into the mushrooms and flour mixture, a little at a time, until smooth. Slowly bring to the boil, stirring all the time, until the sauce boils and thickens. Reduce the heat and simmer for 10 minutes. Add the smetana or crème fraîche and simmer for a further 5 minutes. Season with salt and pepper to taste.

4 Meanwhile, prepare the potato purée. Peel and cut the potatoes into chunks. Put in a pan of salted cold water, bring to the boil then reduce the heat and simmer for 15–20 minutes, until soft. Drain, return to the pan and mash the potatoes until smooth. Add the warm milk, stirring all the time, until the purée is smooth. Add the butter, stir until melted then season with salt.

5 Put the minced chicken, egg, salt and pepper into a bowl and mix well. Form the mixture into eight to ten burgers. Spread the breadcrumbs on to a plate. Turn the burgers in the breadcrumbs until coated and then place them on a plate.

6 Heat the butter in a large frying pan until melted. Add the burgers and fry, in batches if necessary, for about 3 minutes on each side. When all the burgers are cooked, return them to the pan, cover with a lid or folded aluminium foil, and cook over low heat for a further 5 minutes. Serve with the mushroom sauce and potato purée.

Energy 588kcal/2479kJ; Protein 46.6g; Carbohydrate 61.6g, of which sugars 7.3g; Fat 19g, of which saturates 7.8g; Cholesterol 178mg; Calcium 131mg; Fibre 3.3g; Sodium 331mg.

Chicken Kiev
Kotlety pa Kievski s

These classic Ukrainian chicken breasts, filled with garlic butter and then deep-fried, are often accompanied with mushroom sauce. Traditionally the sauce is served in little pastry shells, called croustades, placed on individual serving plates.

Serves 4

4 skinless chicken breast fillets
65g/2½oz/5 tbsp cold butter
1.5ml/¼ tsp ground white pepper
2.5ml/½ tsp garlic powder
150g/5oz/3 cups fresh white breadcrumbs
2–3 eggs
750ml/1¼ pints/3 cups rapeseed
  (canola) oil
salt
cooked rice and sugarsnap peas, to serve

For the mushroom sauce

250g/9oz fresh porcini
25g/1oz/2 tbsp butter
15ml/1 tbsp plain white
  (all-purpose) flour
300ml/½ pint/1¼ cups whipping cream
salt and ground black pepper

COOK'S TIPS
Prepare the chicken parcels well in advance to allow them to chill in the refrigerator before frying. You can also freeze the chicken parcels and then cook them from frozen. Preheat the oven to 180°C/350°F/Gas 4. Deep-fry the parcels for about 10 minutes, until golden brown, then transfer to a baking sheet and bake in the oven for 20 minutes.

1 On the underside of the chicken breast fillets, separate the small finger-thick fillets from the larger fillets. Put one fillet at a time on a sheet of oiled clear film (plastic wrap). Cover with another sheet of clear film and beat with a wooden rolling pin until the large fillets are 5mm/¼in thick and the smaller fillets 3mm/⅛in thick. When flat, remove from the clear film and put on a board.

2 Cut the butter into four sticks. Put the white pepper, garlic powder and 1.5ml/¼ tsp salt on a plate and mix together. Roll the butter sticks in the mixture and place one stick in the centre of each large fillet. Cover with a small flattened fillet and fold the edges of the large fillet up and around to form a tight parcel that holds together. If necessary, secure each parcel with a cocktail stick (toothpick). Sprinkle the parcels with salt. Chill until ready to cook.

3 To make the mushroom sauce, chop the mushrooms. Put in a pan and cook over a medium heat, stirring frequently, until most of the liquid has absorbed. Turn up the heat, add the butter and stir-fry the mushrooms for 5–10 minutes. Sprinkle the flour into the mushrooms and stir until mixed. Gradually stir in the cream, a little at a time, until smooth. Slowly bring to the boil, stirring, until the sauce boils. Reduce the heat and simmer for 10 minutes. Season to taste.

4 Meanwhile, preheat the oven to 220°C/425°F/Gas 7. Line a baking sheet with foil. Spread the breadcrumbs on a plate. Lightly beat the eggs in a small bowl. Brush the chicken parcels with the beaten eggs then roll in the breadcrumbs to coat on all sides. Brush again with the beaten eggs and roll again in the breadcrumbs until evenly coated.

5 Heat the oil in a deep fryer to 180°C/350°F or until a cube of bread browns in 1 minute. Add the chicken parcels to the hot oil and deep-fry for 3–4 minutes, until golden brown. Remove from the pan and place on the prepared baking sheet. Fold in the foil to cover. Bake in the oven for 5–10 minutes. Serve with cooked rice, sugarsnap peas and the mushroom sauce.

Energy 938kcal/3901kJ; Protein 46.2g; Carbohydrate 31.5g, of which sugars 3.3g; Fat 70.7g, of which saturates 33.9g; Cholesterol 327mg; Calcium 122mg; Fibre 1.5g; Sodium 568mg.

Serves 4–6
4 chicken breast fillets, total weight
  500g/1¼lb
500ml/17fl oz/generous 2 cups water
5ml/1 tsp salt
45ml/3 tbsp rapeseed (canola) oil
2 onions, chopped
2 garlic cloves, finely chopped
100g/3¾oz/1 cup walnut halves, plus
  5–6 halves, to garnish
5ml/1 tsp ground coriander
pinch of cayenne pepper
45ml/3 tbsp finely chopped fresh
  coriander (cilantro), to garnish

Chicken with Walnut Sauce Sacivi

VARIATION
Sacivi can also be made with a firm white fish such as halibut.

Sacivi is a Georgian dish, with a lovely sauce of walnuts, which are often picked locally. You need to make this a day in advance to give the chicken time to chill.

1 Put the chicken in a medium pan and pour over enough cold water to cover. Bring to the boil, reduce the heat and simmer for 5 minutes, skimming the surface if necessary. Add the salt, cover and cook for a further 15 minutes.

2 Heat the oil in a small frying pan. Add the chopped onions and garlic and fry for 5 minutes, until softened but not browned.

3 Transfer the onion and garlic to a food processor. Add the walnuts, coriander and cayenne pepper and half of the stock from the chicken. Process until a smooth paste is formed. Add the remaining stock, a little at a time, until it reaches the consistency of a thick sauce. Transfer to a large bowl.

4 Cut the cooked chicken into 3cm/1¼in chunks. Add to the sauce and stir until the chicken is coated in the sauce. Cover and chill overnight.

5 To serve, turn the chicken into a serving dish. Garnish with walnut halves and chopped coriander.

Energy 285kcal/1187kJ; Protein 23.7g; Carbohydrate 7.4g, of which sugars 5.3g; Fat 18.1g, of which saturates 1.8g; Cholesterol 58mg; Calcium 58mg; Fibre 2.2g; Sodium 384mg.

Serves 4–6
1 goose
8–10 Granny Smith apples, peeled, cored
   and cut into wedges
65g/2½oz/5 tbsp butter
200ml/7fl oz/scant 1 cup water
salt and ground black pepper
boiled or roasted potatoes with fresh dill,
   Sauerkraut Stew or boiled buckwheat,
   to serve

Roast Goose with Apples
Utka s Jablokami

In Russia it is traditional to serve your guests roast
goose with apples on New Year's Eve. The goose is
served on a silver plate and carved at the table.

COOK'S TIP
If serving roast potatoes, cook 12 medium
par-boiled potatoes in the oven with the
goose for the last 40 minutes. The
Sauerkraut Stew can also be cooked at
the same time but, if you do, do not
add the prunes.

1 Preheat the oven to 180°C/350°F/
Gas 4. Season the goose inside and
out. Peel, core and quarter four of
the apples and stuff them inside the
neck end of the goose. Fold the neck
skin over then truss the goose,
making sure that the legs are close
to the body. Weigh the goose to work
out cooking time, and calculate
15 minutes per 450g/1lb, plus a
further 15 minutes.

2 Grease a roasting pan with 25g/
1oz/2 tbsp of the butter. Melt the rest
of the butter. Put the goose in the
pan and brush with the melted butter.
Pour the water around the goose.

3 Bake in the oven for 1½ hours,
basting occasionally. Remove the
cores from the remaining apples. Put
the whole apples around the goose
and bake for the remainder of the
cooking time. The goose is cooked
when a skewer is pierced into the
thickest part of a leg and the juices
come out clear.

4 Transfer the goose to a platter.
Remove the stuffing, carve, and serve
with the potatoes and Sauerkraut Stew.

Energy 822kcal/3437kJ; Protein 54.8g; Carbohydrate 44.1g, of which sugars 21.8g; Fat 48.7g, of which saturates 0.9g; Cholesterol 0mg; Calcium 87mg; Fibre 3.1g; Sodium 486mg.

VEGETARIAN AND SIDE DISHES

Cheese Dumplings

Potato Cakes with
Mushroom Sauce

Little Deep-fried Potato Pies

Puff Pastry Cabbage Pie

Fried Mushrooms with
Root Vegetables

Fried Potatoes with Eggs
and Onions

Sauerkraut Stew with Prunes

Vegetable Ragoût

Sauerkraut Salad with
Cranberries

Fresh Spring Salad

Courgettes with Smetana

Russian harvests

Despite their appetite for meat, Russians have been very inventive when it comes to vegetable dishes. Many of these recipes work well either to accompany the main course, or as main courses in their own right. For example, the wide variety of dishes based on the humble potato can easily satisfy a hungry vegetarian. The recipe for Potato Cakes with Mushroom Sauce is a classic and needs only a salad as accompaniment, or perhaps a tasty Vegetable Ragoût. Many recipes for vegetable pies are based on yeast dough and would have been baked in the oven or deep-fried on the hotplate. As in most Eastern European countries, sauerkraut is a favourite. This sharp mixture of fermented cabbage with vinegar makes a very satisfying stew for a cold day, or a light salad for warmer weather. Perhaps the best-loved vegetables after cabbage are mushrooms, which grow wild in the forests and woods of rural Russia. These freely available vegetables crop up in many recipes where their earthy flavour adds depth to blander vegetables.

Serves 4
500g/1¼lb/2½ cups ricotta cheese or
   cottage cheese
2 eggs
200g/7oz/1¾ cups plain white
   (all-purpose) flour
2 litres/3½ pints/8 cups water
25g/1oz/2 tbsp butter
salt
smetana or crème fraîche, to serve

COOK'S TIPS
When the dumplings have been boiled,
it is important to rinse them under cold
running water straight away for a couple
of seconds. This is partly to stop them
cooking, and also to rinse off some of the
starch and stop them from sticking
together. Serve these dumplings with
fried bacon for non-vegetarians, or as a
dessert with smetana and sugar.

Cheese Dumplings
Lenivye Vareniki

Cottage cheese, Italian ricotta, or another fresh cheese
combines well in these delicate but simple Russian
dumplings, which are very similar to Italian gnocchi.

1 Put the cheese, eggs and a pinch of
salt in a bowl and mix well together.
Add the flour and fold in until it is
thoroughly combined. The dough
should be soft and form into a ball.
Remove the ball from the bowl and
put on a floured surface or board.

2 Cut the dough into eight equal pieces
and roll each piece into a sausage
shape about as thick as a finger. Cut
each sausage into 2cm/¾in sections.

3 Bring a large pan of water to the
boil and add 5ml/1 tsp salt. Put half
of the dumplings in the pan and
simmer for 2 minutes, until they float
to the surface. Using a slotted spoon,
remove the dumplings from the pan,
transfer to a colander and put under
cold running water for a few seconds.
Repeat with the second batch of
dumplings in the same way.

4 Heat the butter in a large pan.
Add the drained dumplings and
sauté them until thoroughly warmed
through and slightly golden. Serve
immediately with a bowl of smetana
or crème fraîche.

Energy 803kcal/3328kJ; Protein 11.8g; Carbohydrate 38.9g, of which sugars 0.8g; Fat 68g, of which saturates 41.3g; Cholesterol 227mg; Calcium 208mg; Fibre 1.6g; Sodium 450mg.

Serves 4

1kg/2¼lb floury potatoes
50g/2oz/¼ cup butter
100ml/3½fl oz/scant ½ cup warm milk
1 egg
75g/3oz/1½ cups fresh white
   breadcrumbs
15ml/1 tbsp rapeseed (canola) oil
salt
1 quantity of Mushroom Sauce
   (see page 86) to serve

Potato Cakes with Mushroom Sauce
Kartofeljnye Korlety s Gribnym Sousom

Potatoes are the perfect accompaniment to many Russian dishes and are served fried, boiled, mashed and in gratins, with fish, meat or vegetables. Russians believe potatoes and mushrooms make the perfect combination, and those who do not pick their own mushrooms dry bought ones at home and thread them on a string.

1 Peel and cut the potatoes into even pieces. Put in a pan of salted water, bring to the boil then reduce the heat and simmer for 20 minutes, until soft. Drain, return to the pan and mash until smooth.

2 Add 15g/½oz/1 tbsp of the butter and the milk to the potatoes and mix together until smooth. Leave to cool, then add the the egg and mix together. Season the potatoes with salt to taste.

3 Wet your hands under cold water, take a handful of the mashed potato and form into a cake. Repeat with the remainy mashed potato to make eight cakes. Spread the breadcrumbs on a plate and turn the cakes in the breadcrumbs to coat on both sides. Set aside.

4 To cook the potato cakes, heat the remaining 40g/1½oz/3 tbsp butter and the oil in a large frying pan, add the cakes and fry over a medium heat, for about 3–5 minutes on each side, turning once, until they are golden brown.

5 Gently warm the Mushroom Sauce, and serve the potato cakes hot, accompanied by the sauce.

Energy 389kcal/1637kJ; Protein 8.9g; Carbohydrate 56g, of which sugars 5g; Fat 16g, of which saturates 7.7g; Cholesterol 76mg; Calcium 79mg; Fibre 2.9g; Sodium 274mg.

Little Deep-fried Potato Pies
Jarenye Pirojki s Kartoshkoj

Pirojki are an indispensable part of the zakuski table, but can also be served as accompaniments to soup, when a little hole is made in the top and a spoonful of soup is poured in. Pirojki can be baked, but here they are fried so the pastry is deliciously crisp.

Makes 24
Serves 6–8
For the dough
50g/2oz/¼ cup butter
200ml/7fl oz/scant 1 cup milk
1 small (US medium) egg plus 1 egg yolk
2.5ml/½ tsp salt
7.5ml/1½ tsp caster (superfine) sugar
5g/⅛oz easy-blend (rapid-rise) dried yeast
400g/14oz/3½ cups plain white
  (all-purpose) flour
45ml/3 tbsp water
rapeseed (canola) oil for frying

For the filling
500g/1¼lb floury potatoes
45–60ml/3–4 tbsp rapeseed (canola) oil
2 onions, finely chopped
salt and ground black pepper

COOK'S TIP
The dough can be made in an electric mixer, fitted with a dough hook, if wished.

1 To make the filling, peel and cut the potatoes, put in a pan of salted cold water, bring to the boil then reduce the heat and simmer for 15–20 minutes, until soft. Drain, return to the pan then leave for 2–3 minutes to allow the steam to evaporate. Mash the potatoes until smooth then transfer to a bowl.

2 Heat the oil in a small frying pan, add the onions and fry, stirring frequently, for about 5 minutes until softened and golden brown. Add the onions to the mashed potatoes and mix. Season with plenty of salt and pepper. Set aside.

3 To make the dough, melt the butter in a pan. Add the milk and water and heat it to 45°C/110°F. Remove from the heat. Whisk the whole egg in a large bowl with the salt and sugar. Add the warm milk mixture. Mix the yeast with the flour and stir, a little at a time, into the warm egg mixture. Knead the dough in the bowl for 5 minutes. Cover with a dish towel and leave the dough to rise in a warm place for 30 minutes, until it has doubled in size.

4 Grease a large baking sheet. Turn the dough on to a lightly floured surface and knead for 2–3 minutes. Cut the dough in 24 equal-sized pieces and form each piece into a ball. Leave to rest for 5–10 minutes. Flatten each ball to a round measuring 10cm/4in in diameter.

5 Spread 25ml/1½ tbsp of the potato filling in the centre of each round of dough. Fold together and seal the edges at the top. Put them, upside-down with the join facing down, on a floured wooden chopping board.

6 Half fill a deep pan with oil, and heat to 180°C/350°F, or until a small piece of dough when dropped in, rises to the surface immediately. In batches of around four or five, fry the pies in the oil for 2–3 minutes, turn them over gently, and then cook for a further 2–3 minutes, until golden brown. Remove the pies from the pan with a slotted spoon, and place on kitchen paper to drain. Cook all the pies in this way, and serve immediately.

Energy 349kcal/1467kJ; Protein 8.5g; Carbohydrate 55.1g, of which sugars 6.3g; Fat 12g, of which saturates 4.6g; Cholesterol 64mg; Calcium 127mg; Fibre 3.1g; Sodium 69mg.

Serves 4–6
300–400g/11–14oz cabbage
40–50g/1½–2oz/3–4 tbsp butter
3 eggs
1 sheet ready-made chilled puff pastry,
  measuring about 40x20cm/16x8in
salt

For the glaze
1 egg yolk
5ml/1 tsp water
15ml/1 tbsp fresh white breadcrumbs

COOK'S TIP
This pie is made with one large sheet of
ready-made puff pastry, which can be
bought chilled in one roll. The size should
be about 40x20cm/16x8in. However, if
your sheets are smaller, it is possible to
put three smaller sheets together and
seal them into one large one.

Puff Pastry Cabbage Pie
Pirog Sloenyj s Kapustoj

Crisp puff pastry with a very soft cabbage filling, is a
favourite dish for Russians to eat on a Saturday night
when the whole family is gathered around the table.

1 Discard the outer leaves and hard
stalk of the cabbage, cut in half and
chop finely. Heat the butter in a
medium frying pan over a low heat,
add the cabbage and stir-fry for
25 minutes until softened, don't allow
it to brown. Season and leave to cool.

2 Put the eggs in a pan, cover with
cold water and bring to the boil.
Reduce the heat, and simmer for
10 minutes, then drain and put under
cold running water. Remove the
shells from the eggs then chop and
put in a large bowl. Add the cabbage
to the bowl and mix.

3 Preheat the oven to 220ºC/425ºF/
Gas 7. Put the sheet of pastry on a
dampened baking tray. Spread the

cabbage and egg mixture lengthways
on one half of the pastry sheet.
Brush the edges with water and fold
the other side over to enclose. Seal
together by pressing with a fork
along the join. It should look like a
tightly packed loaf.

4 To make the glaze, whisk together
the egg yolk and water. Brush the
pastry with the mixture and make
some small holes in the top with a
fork. Sprinkle the top of the pastry
with the breadcrumbs.

5 Bake the pie in the oven for
12–15 minutes, until the pastry is
crisp and golden brown. Leave the
baked pie to rest for 5–10 minutes
then cut into portions and serve.

Energy 333kcal/1388kJ; Protein 7.9g; Carbohydrate 25.3g, of which sugars 3.3g; Fat 23.6g, of which saturates 4.5g; Cholesterol 143mg; Calcium 80mg; Fibre 1.2g; Sodium 276mg.

Fried Mushrooms with Root Vegetables
Jarennye Griby s Korneplodami i Gribami

Russians check their hand-picked mushrooms carefully and reserve the most beautiful specimens for drying or marinating. The rest are often cut into pieces and fried in butter or used in soup.

Serves 4
350g/12oz fresh mushrooms, such as porcini, cut into small pieces
65g/2½oz/5 tbsp butter
2 onions, peeled and chopped
1 turnip, finely diced
3 carrots, finely diced
3–4 potatoes, finely diced
60–75ml/4–5 tbsp finely chopped fresh parsley
100ml/3½fl oz/scant ½ cup smetana or crème fraîche
salt and ground black pepper

1 Heat a large frying pan, add the mushrooms and cook over a medium heat, stirring frequently, until all liquid has evaporated. Add half of the butter and the onions and stir-fry for 10 minutes.

2 In a separate frying pan, heat the remaining butter until melted. Add the turnip, carrots and potatoes, in two or three batches, and fry for 10–15 minutes, until softened and golden brown.

3 Mix the mushrooms and the fried root vegetables together, cover the pan and cook for about 10 minutes, until the vegetables are just tender. Season to taste.

4 Sprinkle the chopped parsley into the pan. Stir in the smetana or crème fraîche and reheat gently. Serve hot.

Energy 361kcal/1503kJ; Protein 5.8g; Carbohydrate 31g, of which sugars 11.1g; Fat 24.7g, of which saturates 15.5g; Cholesterol 63mg; Calcium 94mg; Fibre 5.7g; Sodium 150mg.

Serves 4

6–8 potatoes, total weight 1kg/2¼lb,
   peeled and cut into slices or
   thin wedges
60–75ml/4–5 tbsp sunflower oil
50g/2oz/¼ cup butter
1–2 onions, sliced into rings
4 eggs
salt
4 Salted Cucumbers, sliced, and smetana
   or crème fraîche, to serve

Fried Potatoes with Eggs and Onions
Jarennaja Kartoshka s Lukom

A large pan with fried potatoes and onions can make a whole meal for a Russian family,
often served with smetana, bread, Salted Cucumbers and maybe a couple of fried eggs.
Fried potatoes are also the most common accompaniment to Russian fish and meat dishes.

1 Pat the sliced potatoes dry with
kitchen paper. Heat the oil in a very
large frying pan, add the potatoes
and fry for 3 minutes. Shake the pan
or turn the potatoes and fry for a
further 5–10 minutes, until golden.

2 Cover the pan with a lid, or with a
double thickness of foil, and cook
over a low heat for 5–10 minutes,
until the potatoes are tender.

3 Meanwhile, heat 25g/1oz/2 tbsp of
the butter in a small frying pan, add the
onions and fry, stirring frequently, for
5–10 minutes until golden brown.
Mix the fried onions with the cooked
potatoes and season with salt.

4 Wipe out the frying pan that the
onions were cooked in and melt the
remaining butter in the pan. Break
each egg into the pan and fry, basting
with the butter, so the eggs cook
evenly on top and underneath. When
set, remove from the pan and place
on top of the potatoes. Serve with
Salted Cucumbers and smetana or
crème fraîche.

Energy 477kcal/1990kJ; Protein 11.8g; Carbohydrate 48.2g, of which sugars 8.9g; Fat 27.8g, of which saturates 9.6g; Cholesterol 217mg; Calcium 71mg; Fibre 3.9g; Sodium 176mg.

Serves 4

700g/1lb 10oz sauerkraut
2 large onions
75–100g/3–3¾oz/6–7½ tbsp butter
5 black peppercorns
1 bay leaf
1 whole garlic bulb, about 10 cloves
200ml/7fl oz/scant 1 cup water
15ml/1 tbsp sugar
8 dried prunes
salt

Sauerkraut Stew with Prunes
Kapusta Tuschenaja s Chernoslivom

Dried fruits are often used in Russian cuisine, not only for desserts but also in main courses. In this dish they add a delicious sweetness to the contrasting sour taste of the sauerkraut. Serve the dish as a main course with potatoes or to accompany baked ham.

1 Preheat the oven to 200°C/400°F/ Gas 6. Rinse the sauerkraut under running water if you find it too sour. Chop the onions. Heat the butter in a medium pan. Add the onions and fry for 5–8 minutes, stirring occasionally, until soft and golden brown. Add the sauerkraut and fork it through to mix with the fried onions and butter.

2 Add the peppercorns and bay leaf to the sauerkraut and onion mixture. Add the garlic bulb, without peeling or separating into cloves.

3 Transfer the sauerkraut mixture into an ovenproof dish. Add the water and sugar, and season with salt.

4 Bake the sauerkraut in the oven for 30 minutes, stirring occasionally. After 30 minutes, stir in the prunes. Return to the oven and bake for a further 20 minutes, stirring two or three times during cooking.

COOK'S TIP
Sauerkraut is available bottled or canned from large supermarkets.

Energy 239kcal/986kJ; Protein 4.2g; Carbohydrate 21.2g, of which sugars 18.3g; Fat 15.7g, of which saturates 9.8g; Cholesterol 40mg; Calcium 142mg; Fibre 7g; Sodium 1298mg.

Serves 4
3–4 carrots
1 swede (rutabaga)
1 turnip
1 parsnip
10ml/2 tsp sunflower oil
1 large onion, finely chopped
100–200ml/3½–7fl oz/scant ½–1 cup
  vegetable stock or lightly salted water
105ml/7 tbsp finely chopped fresh parsley
15g/½oz/1 tbsp butter
dark rye bread and butter, to serve

Vegetable Ragoût
Ragu iz Ovocshej

VARIATION
Add 100g/3¾oz/scant 1 cup fresh or
frozen peas to the ragoût 3 minutes
before adding the chopped fresh parsley
and butter.

Russians prefer to eat their vegetables very soft and very
hot. Both are illustrated in this recipe. Serve the ragoût
with dark rye bread and a little butter.

1 Cut the carrots, swede, turnip and
parsnip into small chunks. Heat the
oil in a flameproof casserole, add the
chopped onion and fry over a medium
heat, for 3–5 minutes until softened.

2 Add the carrots, swede, turnip and
parsnip to the pan and fry, stirring
frequently, for a further 10 minutes. Add
the stock and bring to the boil. Cover
with a lid and simmer for 20 minutes
until the vegetables are soft.

3 Add the chopped parsley and the
butter to the pan and stir until
the butter has melted. Season with
salt to taste and serve hot.

Energy 122kcal/506kJ; Protein 2.6g; Carbohydrate 15.9g, of which sugars 13.3g; Fat 5.7g, of which saturates 2.3g; Cholesterol 8mg; Calcium 137mg; Fibre 6.3g; Sodium 68mg.

Serves 4–6
500g/1¼lb sauerkraut
2 red apples
100–200g/3¾–7oz/scant 1–1¾ cups fresh
  cranberries or lingonberries
30ml/2 tbsp sugar
60–75ml/4–5 tbsp sunflower oil
2–3 sprigs fresh parsley, to garnish

Sauerkraut Salad with Cranberries
Salat iz Kisloj Kapusty s Kljukvoj

Cabbage is a staple ingredient in Russia and the best soured cabbage can be bought in the market halls, where you are invited to taste both the cabbage and the brine. It is not unusual for a customer to taste up to ten different kinds before making a decision.

1 Put the sauerkraut in a colander and drain thoroughly. Taste, and if you find it is too sour, rinse it under cold running water then drain well.

2 Put the sauerkraut in a large bowl. Slice or cut the apples into slices or wedges. Add the apples and the cranberries or lingonberries to the sauerkraut. Sprinkle over the sugar, pour the oil on top and mix all the ingredients well together.

3 To serve, turn the sauerkraut into a serving bowl and garnish with the parsley sprigs.

Energy 105kcal/437kJ; Protein 1.3g; Carbohydrate 8.8g, of which sugars 8.8g; Fat 7.4g, of which saturates 0.9g; Cholesterol 0mg; Calcium 49mg; Fibre 3.1g; Sodium 493mg.

Serves 4
2 eggs
1 large cos or romaine lettuce
1 cucumber
10 radishes
1 bunch spring onions (scallions)
45ml/3 tbsp roughly chopped fresh dill,
　to garnish

For the dressing
200ml/7fl oz/scant 1 cup smetana or
　crème fraîche
juice of 1 lemon
15ml/1 tbsp sugar
pinch of salt

COOK'S TIP
Prepare this salad no more than 1 hour
before serving and add the dressing
just before it is served.

Fresh Spring Salad
Vesennij Salat

This pretty salad can be served as an accompaniment to most meat and fish dishes. It is a typical home-made Russian dish and is hardly ever served in restaurants.

1 First make the dressing so it has time for the flavours to develop. Put the smetana or crème fraîche and lemon juice in a small bowl and whisk together. Add the sugar and salt and stir until the sugar is completely dissolved. Set aside.

2 Put the eggs in a pan, cover with cold water and bring to the boil. Reduce the heat to low, and simmer for 10 minutes. When the eggs are cooked, drain and put under cold running water. Remove the shells and slice the eggs.

3 Using a sharp knife, cut the lettuce into 5–6cm/2–2½in pieces and put in a serving dish. Peel and finely slice the cucumber, slice the radishes, and finely slice the spring onions.

4 Layer the salad by placing the cucumber on top of the shredded lettuce, then the radishes, then the egg and finally the spring onions.

5 Spoon the dressing over the salad and garnish with chopped fresh dill. Serve immediately.

Energy 268kcal/1107kJ; Protein 6g; Carbohydrate 8.7g, of which sugars 8.5g; Fat 23.5g, of which saturates 14.5g; Cholesterol 152mg; Calcium 96mg; Fibre 1.8g; Sodium 55mg.

Serves 4

4 small courgettes (zucchini)
45–75ml/3–5 tbsp plain white
   (all-purpose) flour
30ml/2 tbsp rapeseed (canola) oil
45ml/3 tbsp chopped fresh parsley
200ml/7fl oz/scant 1 cup smetana or
   crème fraîche
salt and ground black pepper
rye bread to serve

Courgettes with Smetana
Kabachki w Smetane

Russians who have their own *dacha* (country house) grow their own vegetables. Courgette plants usually yield a good harvest. They are preserved, salted or marinated, fried and mixed with caviar and also fried and served in a creamy, mild smetana sauce.

1 Cut the courgettes into 1cm/½in thick slices. Coat the slices, on both sides, in the flour.

2 Heat the oil in a large frying pan, then add the courgettes, working in batches if necessary to form a single layer, and fry for about 1 minute on each side or until golden brown. Remove from the pan and keep warm until all the courgettes are fried.

3 Return all the courgettes to the pan. Season the courgettes with salt and pepper and sprinkle with the chopped parsley.

4 Add the smetana or crème fraîche to the pan, cover and simmer over a low heat for about 5 minutes until the courgettes are soft.

5 Serve the courgettes warm, straight from the pan with rye bread.

VARIATION
Aubergines (eggplants) can be cooked in the same way. Slice 2 aubergines, coat in the flour and fry in 60ml/4 tbsp oil. Add the parsley but omit the smetana.

Energy 312kcal/1290kJ; Protein 5.7g; Carbohydrate 13.4g, of which sugars 4.5g; Fat 26.5g, of which saturates 14.4g; Cholesterol 56mg; Calcium 111mg; Fibre 2.5g; Sodium 17mg.

DESSERTS, BAKING AND DRINKS

Sweet and delicious

A Russian meal can be quite filling, but luckily the dessert at the end is always light, and is often made up of several little sweet dishes, rather like the zakuski. These may include little cakes, stewed dried fruit, and perhaps some little pies. Many of these recipes are based on fruit, either the widely available ones such as cherries, blueberries and apples, or more exotic fruits from one of the warmer Soviet republics – grenadines, grapes or watermelon. These are combined in delicious concoctions such as cherry compote, or vanilla ice cream with frozen berries and warm fudge sauce. Pies, cakes and flavoured breads are staple dishes when a more substantial recipe is required, or as the centrepiece of a celebration, such as a religious feast day or birthday. These are often based on yeast dough with spices and fruit fillings. Afternoon tea is a Russian speciality, with plenty of tea – still sometimes served from a samovar – little pots of jam, and perhaps a delicious creamy layer cake, sometimes bought from a bakers but often made at home.

Serves 4

250g/9oz/1¼ cups mixed dried fruits
   including plums, pears, apples
   and apricots
1.5 litres/2½ pints/6¼ cups water
2 cinnamon sticks or bay leaves
60ml/4 tbsp raisins
5ml/1 tsp finely grated lemon or
   orange rind
30–45ml/2–3 tbsp sugar

Dried Fruit Compote
Kompot iz Suchafruktov

Russian suppers almost always consist of three dishes – a soup, the main dish and a dessert. To round off an evening meal, a compote is the most popular final course. You can mix the fruit ingredients to suit your own taste or what is available.

1 Keeping the fruit types separate, cut any large pieces of fruit into smaller chunks. Pour the water into a medium pan and bring to the boil.

2 When the water is boiling, add the plums, pears, cinnamon sticks or bay leaves and return to the boil. Reduce the heat and simmer for 10 minutes.

3 Add the apples and apricots to the pan and simmer for 10 minutes. Add the raisins and simmer for a further 5 minutes.

4 Using a slotted spoon, remove the fruit from the pan and transfer to a heatproof serving bowl.

5 Add the sugar to the juices in the pan, bring to the boil then boil for 5 minutes until it thickens slightly.

6 Pour the syrup over the fruit and serve the compote warm or cold.

COOK'S TIP
In Armenia the compote is flavoured with a little brandy and chopped walnuts and you could do this too.

Energy 169kcal/721kJ; Protein 2.9g; Carbohydrate 41.1g, of which sugars 41.1g; Fat 0.4g, of which saturates 0g; Cholesterol 0mg; Calcium 57mg; Fibre 4.2g; Sodium 18mg.

Serves 6–8
60g/2¼oz/4½ tbsp cold butter
1 egg
150ml/¼ pint/⅔ cup milk
10 slices of 2–3 days old white bread
6–8 apples
130g/4½oz/⅔ cup caster
 (superfine) sugar

Bread and Apple Bake
Scharlotka s Jablokami

Bread has always been the basic, staple food of Russian cuisine. It is treated with great respect, bought fresh each day and used to the last crumb. This recipe makes a new dish out of old bread – frugal, simple but very good.

1 Preheat the oven to 200°C/400°F/Gas 6. Use 10g/¼oz/1½ tsp of the butter to grease a 20cm/8in flan tin (pan). Put the egg and milk in a bowl and whisk together.

2 Cut five bread slices in half. Dip them, one at a time, into the milk mixture and place in the flan tin so that they cover the edges. Dip the remaining uncut bread slices in the milk mixture and place tightly in the bottom of the tin.

3 Cut the remaining 50g/2oz/4 tbsp butter into small cubes. Peel and core the apples and cut the flesh into small pieces.

4 Put half of the apples on top of the bread, sprinkle with half of the sugar then add half of the butter cubes. Top with the remaining apples, sugar and butter.

5 Bake in the oven for 15 minutes. Lower the temperature to 180°C/350°F/Gas 4 and bake for a further 35 minutes, until golden brown. Serve warm, straight from the tin.

Energy 245kcal/1038kJ; Protein 4.6g; Carbohydrate 41.8g, of which sugars 26.1g; Fat 7.9g, of which saturates 4.3g; Cholesterol 41mg; Calcium 77mg; Fibre 1.6g; Sodium 240mg.

Baked Cheesecake
Zapekanka iz Tvoroga

Russians love their tea and tea drinking is an ancient Russian tradition. It is popular to have parties where nothing but tea and sweet accompaniments are served. These include cherry jam, gooseberry jam and whole strawberry jam (put in the tea or eaten from special small plates), chocolates, fudge and soft spicy ginger cookies. The highlight of the tea is a cheesecake, flavoured with raisins, preserved peel and lemon.

Serves 6–8

15g/½oz/1 tbsp butter
45ml/3 tbsp fresh white breadcrumbs
4 eggs
100g/3¾oz mixed (candied) peel
500g/1¼lb/2 cups cottage or ricotta
  cheese
90g/3½oz/½ cup caster (superfine) sugar
50g/2oz/scant ½ cup raisins
grated rind of 1 lemon
45ml/3 tbsp semolina
icing (confectioners') sugar, for dusting
smetana, crème fraîche or whipped
  cream, and fresh berries, such as
  strawberries, raspberries, blueberries
  or redcurrants, to serve

1 Preheat the oven to 180ºC/350ºF/Gas 4. Use the butter to grease the bottom and sides of a 20cm/8in loose-bottomed cake tin (pan) then pour in the breadcrumbs and tip and shake until the insides of the tin are well coated with the breadcrumbs.

2 Separate the egg yolks from the egg whites into two separate large bowls. Finely chop the candied peel and add to the egg yolks. Add the cottage or ricotta cheese, sugar, raisins, lemon rind and semolina and mix well together.

3 Whisk the egg whites until they are stiff and hold their shape then carefully fold into the cheese mixture. Spoon the mixture into the prepared tin.

4 Bake the cake in the oven for 30–40 minutes, until a skewer, inserted in the centre, comes out dry. Leave the cake to cool in the tin.

5 Slide a knife around the edge of the cake and carefully remove it from the tin. Place on a serving plate and dust with sifted icing sugar.

6 Serve the cheesecake with smetana or crème fraîche or whipped cream and fresh berries.

Energy 297kcal/1239kJ; Protein 7.6g; Carbohydrate 27.2g, of which sugars 19g; Fat 18g, of which saturates 9g; Cholesterol 83mg; Calcium 56mg; Fibre 1.1g; Sodium 139mg.

Serves 4–6
5–6 cooking apples
40–50g/1½–2oz/3–4 tbsp butter
45ml/3 tbsp raisins
1 sheet ready-made chilled puff pastry,
   measuring about 40x20cm/16x8in
1 egg yolk
5ml/1 tsp water

COOK'S TIP
If your sheets of pastry are smaller
than the sheet specified in the recipe,
put three smaller sheets together and
seal them into one large sheet.

Apple Pie
Pirog Sloenyj s Jablokami

Russians like to finish the day with *vechernij chaj* –
evening tea. Chocolate confectionary, cookies, berries
and spoonfuls of jam may be served. If something more
substantial is required, a large home-baked pie is served
with the steaming hot tea.

1 Slice the apples, discarding the
cores. Put the butter in a medium
frying pan and heat until melted. Add
the apples and stir-fry, over a low
heat, for 5 minutes, until soft.

2 Remove the pan from the heat, add
the raisins and mix together. Set
aside and leave to cool.

3 Preheat the oven to 220ºC/425ºF/
Gas 7. Put the sheet of pastry on a
dampened baking tray. Distribute the
apple filling over the pastry, leaving a
5cm/2in border around the edge.

4 Brush the edges of the pastry with
water or milk and fold over to
enclose the filling.

5 Whisk the egg yolk and water
together. Brush the pastry with the
mixture and make some small holes
in the top with a fork.

6 Bake the pie in the oven for
12–15 minutes, until golden brown.
Allow the pie to rest for 5–10 minutes
then cut into slices and serve with a
spoonful of smetana or crème fraîche.

Energy 393kcal/1650kJ; Protein 4.1g; Carbohydrate 56.3g, of which sugars 27.7g; Fat 18.4g, of which saturates 11.4g; Cholesterol 46mg; Calcium 68mg; Fibre 2.5g; Sodium 136mg.

Serves 4
4 large, firm apples
15g/½oz/1 tbsp butter
vanilla ice cream, to serve

For the filling
25g/1oz/2 tbsp butter
90ml/6 tbsp blanched almonds
   or hazelnuts
30ml/2 tbsp sugar
5ml/1 tsp ground cinnamon

Baked Apples with Cinnamon and Nuts
Pechjonye Jabloki s Koricej i Orehami

Cream cake may be one of the most popular desserts in Russia, but health conscious young Russians of today appreciate lighter desserts and are as happy to serve baked apples – another old traditional Russian classic dessert.

1 Preheat the oven to 220°C/425°F/ Gas 7. To make the filling, melt the butter. Grind or finely chop the almonds or hazelnuts and put in a bowl. Add the sugar, cinnamon and melted butter and mix together.

2 Using a vegetable peeler, peel the apples. Using a corer or a small spoon, remove the cores, leaving the apples intact at the bottom to ensure that the filling will not run out. Put the apples in an ovenproof dish.

3 Divide the filling into four, and stuff the apples with a portion each. Melt the butter in a small pan and pour over the apples to coat.

4 Bake the apples in the oven for about 20 minutes, until the apples are soft, but before they collapse. Serve hot, with vanilla ice cream.

VARIATION
Instead of flavouring with cinnamon, use the same quantity of ground cardamom or vanilla extract.

Energy 294kcal/1229kJ; Protein 5.3g; Carbohydrate 22.8g, of which sugars 22.2g; Fat 20.9g, of which saturates 6.2g; Cholesterol 21mg; Calcium 66mg; Fibre 4.1g; Sodium 67mg.

Small Blueberry Pies
Vatrushki s Chernikoj

Delicious little blueberry pies are perfect as a dessert after a Sunday lunch. Alternatively, serve them in the afternoon; seat your guests in the garden and bring out the samovar. Serve these home-made temptations on a Russian tray decorated with beautiful fresh flowers, with lots of hot tea.

Makes 10

For the dough
50g/2oz/¼ cup butter
200ml/7fl oz/scant 1 cup milk
45ml/3 tbsp water
2.5ml/½ tsp salt
7.5ml/1½ tsp caster (superfine) sugar
1 small (US medium) egg
400g/14oz/3½ cups plain white
  (all-purpose) flour
large pinch of easy-blend (rapid-rise)
  dried yeast

For the filling
300–350g/11–12oz/2¾–3 cups
  blueberries, fresh or frozen
25g/1oz/2 tbsp caster (superfine) sugar
15ml/1 tbsp potato flour

For the glaze
150ml/¼ pint/⅔ cup smetana or
  crème fraîche
45ml/3 tbsp caster (superfine) sugar
icing (confectioners') sugar, for dusting

1 To make the dough, melt the butter in a small pan. Add the milk, water, salt and sugar and heat until warm to the finger. Pour the mixture into a large bowl. Add the egg and mix together.

2 Put the flour and yeast in a large bowl and mix together. Stir in the butter mixture, a little at a time, until combined. Knead the dough in the bowl for at least 5 minutes. Cover the bowl with a dish towel and leave the dough to rise in a warm place for 30 minutes until it has doubled in size.

3 Turn the dough on to a lightly floured surface. Cut the dough into 24 equal-sized pieces and form each piece into a ball. Leave to rest for 5–10 minutes.

4 Meanwhile, prepare the filling. Put the blueberries in a bowl, add the sugar and potato flour and mix together.

5 Preheat the oven to 200°C/400°F/Gas 6. Grease a large baking tray. Flatten each ball to a round measuring about 15cm/6in in diameter.

6 Place the rounds on the baking tray. Place 45ml/3 tbsp of the blueberry mixture in the centre of each round then fold a small edge up around the mixture. Bake the pies in the oven for 10–15 minutes, until golden brown.

7 Meanwhile, make the glaze. Put the smetana or crème fraîche and the sugar in a bowl and mix together.

8 When the pies are baked, gently spoon a little of the glaze over each pie. Dust the tops with sifted icing sugar. Serve hot or cold.

Energy 371kcal/1559kJ; Protein 4.4g; Carbohydrate 55.8g, of which sugars 25.7g; Fat 16g, of which saturates 4.9g; Cholesterol 8mg; Calcium 93mg; Fibre 3.2g; Sodium 228mg.

Serves 4
225g/8oz/1 cup cottage cheese or
  ricotta cheese
45ml/3 tbsp plain white
  (all-purpose) flour
1 egg, plus 1 egg yolk
30ml/2 tbsp vanilla sugar
15ml/1 tbsp icing (confectioners') sugar
30ml/2 tbsp rapeseed (canola) oil
whipped double (heavy) cream, smetana
  or crème fraîche and fresh berries,
  such as raspberries, blueberries or
  redcurrants, to serve

Cottage Cheese Pancakes
Oladyshki iz Tvoraga

Crispy and delicious, these little pancakes are very
popular in Russia as a dessert. They are traditionally
served warm, with fresh berries and smetana.

1 Put the cottage or ricotta cheese in
a food processor. Add the flour, egg
yolk, vanilla sugar and icing sugar
and process until smooth.

2 Heat the oil in a non-stick frying
pan, over a medium heat. Pour a
tablespoon of the batter into the pan,
adding another one or two spoonfuls,
depending on the space in the pan.

3 Fry the pancakes for 1 minute then,
using a metal spatula, flip them and
cook the other side for a further
1 minute.

4 Transfer the pancakes to a warmed
plate and keep warm until you have
cooked all the batter.

5 Serve warm with smetana or
crème fraîche and decorate with
fresh berries.

COOK'S TIP
You can prepare the pancakes in advance
and heat them in the oven at 110ºC/
225ºF/Gas ¼ for about 5 minutes, until
warm, before serving.

Energy 171kcal/716kJ; Protein 4.2g; Carbohydrate 20.7g, of which sugars 12.1g; Fat 8.5g, of which saturates 1.5g; Cholesterol 98mg; Calcium 39mg; Fibre 0.4g; Sodium 45mg.

Serves 4

50g/2oz/¼ cup butter
3 eggs
2.5ml/½ tsp salt
2ml/⅓ tsp caster (superfine) sugar
200ml/7fl oz/scant 1 cup warm water
185g/6½oz/1⅔ cups plain white
   (all-purpose) flour
350ml/12fl oz/1½ cups milk
60–75ml/4–5 tbsp rapeseed (canola)
   oil, for brushing, and 30–45ml/
   2–3 tbsp, for frying
smetana or crème fraîche, and caster
   (superfine) sugar, to serve

For the filling

500g/1¼lb/2½ cups fresh cheese, such as
   ricotta or cottage cheese
2 egg yolks
30–45ml/2–3 tbsp caster (superfine) sugar

Crêpes with a Cheese Filling Blinchiki s Tvorogom

Fresh cheese is an everyday food in Russia and is often eaten on its own. By omitting the sugar, these crêpes can be adapted to a savoury dish for a main course.

1 Melt the butter. Whisk the eggs, salt and sugar together in a bowl. Add the water, then gradually whisk in the flour. Stir in the milk, a little at a time, with the melted butter.

2 Heat a non-stick frying pan over a medium heat. Brush it with a little oil and pour in a thin layer of batter. As soon as the surface has set, turn the crêpe over and cook the other side. Fry the remaining crêpes in the same way, brushing the pan with oil each time and stacking when cooked.

3 To make the filling, put the cottage cheese or ricotta cheese and egg yolks in a bowl and mix together. Add sugar to taste. Place 45ml/3 tbsp of the filling in the centre of each crêpe and fold over to create an envelope.

4 Heat the oil in a frying pan. Add the envelopes, joint-side down, and fry, over a medium heat, for 1–2 minutes. Turn and fry the other sides for 1–2 minutes, until golden brown. Serve the pancakes with smetana or crème fraîche and sugar for sprinkling.

Energy 1054kcal/4371kJ; Protein 17.5g; Carbohydrate 48g, of which sugars 12.7g; Fat 89.6g, of which saturates 47.9g; Cholesterol 394mg; Calcium 332mg; Fibre 1.4g; Sodium 547mg.

Pashka
Pashka

This fresh cheese and dried fruit dessert is made by mixing the ingredients together, putting them in a lined mould and letting all the liquid drain away, creating a firm, dome-shaped pudding. The traditional shape is a pyramid, made in a wooden mould, but a coffee filter-holder or a clean plastic flower pot work equally well. Paskha needs to be made a few days in advance, and is traditionally eaten to celebrate the end of Lent.

Serves 6–8
500g/1¼lb/2½ cups ricotta cheese or
    cottage cheese
75g/3oz/6 tbsp unsalted butter, softened
275g/10oz/1½ cups caster (superfine)
    sugar
30ml/2 tbsp vanilla sugar
150ml/¼ pint/⅔ cup whipping cream
30ml/2 tbsp smetana or crème fraîche
2 egg yolks
40g/1½oz/generous ¼ cup raisins
grated rind 1 lemon
glacé (candied) orange or lemon and
    blanched almonds, to decorate

1 If using cottage cheese, push the cheese through a sieve (strainer). Put the ricotta or cottage cheese in a sieve and stand the sieve over a bowl. Leave to drain overnight in a cold place.

2 Line a clean 750ml/1¼ pints/3 cups coffee filter, or a flower pot with a drainage hole, with damp muslin (cheesecloth) allowing the edges of the muslin to overhang the edges. Transfer the drained cheese into a bowl, add the butter, sugar and vanilla sugar and beat together until smooth.

3 Pour the whipping cream into a separate bowl and whisk until it forms soft peaks. Stir the cream, smetana or crème fraîche and egg yolks into the cheese mixture then whisk until fluffy and smooth. Add the raisins and grated lemon rind and stir together.

4 Spoon the mixture into the lined holder and fold the edges of the muslin into the centre. Cover with a small saucer that fits inside the holder and put a 500g/1¼lb weight on top. Stand in a bowl or soup plate and leave in a cold place, to drain, for one to three days.

5 Remove the weight and saucer. Unfold the muslin and very carefully turn the paskha out on to a serving plate. Remove the muslin. Serve the Paskha decorated with candied fruits and nuts.

Energy 369kcal/1544kJ; Protein 9.3g; Carbohydrate 41.9g, of which sugars 41.9g; Fat 19.1g, of which saturates 11.5g; Cholesterol 100mg; Calcium 118mg; Fibre 0.1g; Sodium 256mg.

Russian Easter Cake Kulitj

A traditional Easter dinner in Russia always starts with zakuski and ends with a home-made kulitj, a high, round cake flavoured with cardamom and vanilla. Kulitj is also served at Easter and between kulitj and paskha one feasts on Easter eggs. Traditionally, the kulitj, pashka and Easter eggs are blessed by the priests.

Serves 8–10

200ml/7fl oz/scant 1 cup milk
350–425g/12–15oz/3–3⅔ cups plain white (all-purpose) flour
185g/6½oz/scant 1 cup caster (superfine) sugar
large pinch easy-blend (rapid-rise) dried yeast
115g/4oz/½ cup butter, plus extra for greasing
15ml/1 tbsp vanilla sugar
2.5ml/½ tsp salt
5ml/1 tsp ground cardamom
3 egg yolks
150g/5oz/1 cup raisins

1 Pour the milk into a small pan and heat until warm to the finger. Remove from the heat. Put 325g/11½oz/scant 3 cups of the flour, half of the sugar and the yeast in a food processor and mix together.

2 Add the warm milk to the processor and mix until combined. Cover and leave to rise in a warm place for about 30 minutes, until doubled in size.

3 Melt the butter. Add the remaining sugar, the vanilla sugar, salt, cardamom and melted butter, reserving 15ml/1 tbsp, to the risen dough and mix together until smooth. Add the egg yolks, one at a time, until combined.

4 Generously grease a 17cm/6½in round, 10cm/4in deep, cake tin (pan) or 1.5 litre/2½ pint/6¼ cup soufflé dish with butter.

5 Transfer the dough to a lightly floured surface and knead in the remaining flour and the raisins. Put the dough into the prepared tin or dish, cover and leave to rise for 30 minutes.

6 Preheat the oven to 180°C/350°F/Gas 4. Brush the dough with half of the reserved melted butter. Bake in the oven for 30 minutes. Brush with the remaining melted butter and bake for a further 20–30 minutes, until risen and golden brown. Remove from the tin or dish and transfer to a wire rack to cool.

COOK'S TIPS
If preferred, the mixture can be made in a large bowl, rather than in a food processor. Cover the cake with baking parchment, halfway through the cooking time, if it shows signs of becoming too brown.

Energy 346kcal/1459kJ; Protein 5.3g; Carbohydrate 57.9g, of which sugars 31.3g; Fat 12g, of which saturates 6.7g; Cholesterol 86mg; Calcium 99mg; Fibre 1.4g; Sodium 92mg.

Makes 2 litres/3½ pints/8 cups
150g/5oz/generous ½ cup honey
100g/3¾oz/generous ½ cup sugar
500ml/17fl oz/generous 2 cups water

For the spice mixture
10ml/2 tsp St John's wort
2 cloves
5–6 black peppercorns
1.5ml/¼ tsp ground ginger
5ml/1 tsp ground cinnamon
10ml/2 tsp dried mint
1 litre/1¾ pints/4 cups water

Spiced Honey Drink
Sbitenj

This spiced drink, made with honey, herbs and spices, is
one of Russia's oldest drinks, and was quite forgotten
during the Soviet era. In old Russia it was sold in the
streets and you could hear the vendors crying its name.
After the perestroika this hot drink has experienced a
renaissance. It complements traditional dishes very well.

1 Put all the ingredients for the spice
mixture in a medium pan.

2 Bring to the boil, then lower the
heat, cover and simmer for
5 minutes, skimming the surface if
necessary. Remove the pan from the
heat and leave to stand.

3 Meanwhile, mix the honey and
sugar in a separate medium pan.

4 Add the water to the honey and
sugar mixture and bring to the boil,
constantly stirring.

5 Lower the heat and simmer the
mixture for 10 minutes, making sure
that it does not boil.

6 Strain the spiced water into the pan
and heat gently, without boiling.
Serve warm.

Energy 558kcal/2374kJ; Protein 5.1g; Carbohydrate 135.5g, of which sugars 125.1g; Fat 3.9g, of which saturates 0.6g; Cholesterol 0mg; Calcium 67mg; Fibre 0g; Sodium 27mg.

Makes 2 litres/3½ pints/8 cups
150g/5oz/generous ½ cup honey
2 litres/3½ pints/8 cups water
large pinch of dried hops
1 cardamom pod
5ml/1 tsp preserving sugar
10g/¼oz fresh yeast

Honey and Cardamom Drink
Medok

It is a well-known fact that Russian gentlemen drink vodka with their food while the women prefer champagne but, for a variation, try this old Russian, alcohol-free honey and cardamom drink as an accompaniment to your Russian meal. Made with spice and honey, it is said to have an invigorating effect.

1 Mix the honey and 350ml/12fl oz/1½ cups of the water in a pan. Bring to the boil, then lower the heat and simmer for 2–3 minutes, skimming the surface if necessary.

2 Mix the dried hops and 150ml/5fl oz/⅔ cup of the water in a separate medium pan. Bring to the boil, then lower the heat and simmer for 2–3 minutes. Add the honey water.

3 Bring the mixture to the boil and add the remaining water. Remove from the heat and leave the liquid to cool at room temperature until it is about 40°C/104°F.

4 Add the cardamom, sugar and yeast to the pan. Cover with a dish towel and set aside at 8–10°C/46–50°F, until the surface is foamy.

5 Skim, drain and pour into clean bottles. Store in the refrigerator and drink within a week. Serve chilled.

Energy 469kcal/1999kJ; Protein 4.2g; Carbohydrate 120.2g, of which sugars 119.8g; Fat 0.1g, of which saturates 0g; Cholesterol 0mg; Calcium 18mg; Fibre 0g; Sodium 22mg.

Useful Addresses

AUSTRALIA
Russian Tidbits
113 Koornang Road,
Carnegie
VIC 3163
Tel: (03) 9572 3911

V & V
136 Koornang Road,
Carnegie
VIC 3163
Tel: (03) 9568 1621

CANADA
Wendy's Gourmet Perogies
4532 99th St NW,
Edmonton
AR T6E 5V6
Tel: 780-432-3893
(restaurant but sells perogies to take away)

NEW ZEALAND
St. Petersburg Restaurant
333 Parnell Road
Parnell
Auckland 1052
Tel: (09) 373 3179

UK
Babushka
12–16 Bridge Street
Mansfield
Nottingham
NG18 1AN
Tel: (07949) 719937
www.babushkadeli.uk

Dacha Delicatessen
34 Aylmer Parade,
East Finchley
London N2 0PE
and 74 Ballards Lane
Finchley Central
London N3 2BU
and 649 Fulham Broadway
London SW6 5PU
Tel: (020) 83 412 475
www.dachashop.co.uk

Erebuni Restaurant
2–5 Carthusian Street
London
EC1M 6EB
Tel: (020) 7253 9319
www.erebuni.co.uk

CCCP Restaurant
14–18 Chatham Street
Ramsgate
CT11 7PP
Tel: 01843592811
www.cccprestaurant.co.uk

USA
skazkarussianfood.com
RussianTable.com
60 20th Street,
Sunset Industrial Park,
Brooklyn
New York
NY 11232
Tel: 718-858-6720
www.russiantable.com
Email: info@russiantable.com

Moscow on the Hudson
801 West 181st Street
New York
NY 10033
Tel: 212-740-7397
www.moscowonhudson.com

Babushkas Deli
491 S Livingston Ave
Livingston
NJ 07039
Tel: (973) 533-0394
www.babushkasdeli.com

Babushka Deli
62 Washington Street
Brighton, MA 02135
Tel: 617-731-9739

Russian Café and Deli
1712 Winchester Blvd
Campbell, CA 95008
Tel: 408-379-6680
www.russiancafedeli.com

Marky's Gourmet Food Store
687 NE 79th Street, Miami, FL 33138
Tel: 305-758-9288
www.markys.com

Slavic Shop
1080 Saratoga Avenue Suite #1, San Jose, CA 95129
Tel: 408-615-8533
www.slavicstores.com

Moscow Deli
3015 Harbor Blvd, Costa Mesa, CA 92626
Tel: 714-429-5920
www.moscowdeli.com

Russian General Store
9629 Hillcroft Street, Houston, TX 77096
Tel: 713-665-1177

Berezka International Food Store
1215 Commonwealth Avenue,
Boston, MA 02134
Tel: 617-787-2837
www.berezkaboston.com

Bz Bee Market
2322 S El Camino Real,
San Mateo, CA 94403
Tel: 650-627-9303

Index